MW01503327

# Good News, Great Joy

## AN ADVENT STUDY ON THE POWER AND PERFECTION OF JESUS

THIS STUDY BELONGS TO:

THE DAILY GRACE CO.®

*Good News, Great Joy | An Advent Study on the Power and Perfection of Jesus*
Copyright © 2023 by The Daily Grace Co.®
Spring, Texas. All rights reserved.

Unless otherwise noted, all Scripture quotations are taken from the Christian Standard Bible®, Copyright © 2020 by Holman Bible Publishers. Used by permission. Christian Standard Bible® and CSB® are federally registered trademarks of Holman Bible Publishers.

Scripture quotations marked (NIV) are taken from the Holy Bible, New International Version®, NIV®. Copyright © 1973, 1978, 1984, 2011 by Biblica, Inc.® Used by permission of Zondervan. All rights reserved worldwide. www.zondervan.com The "NIV" and "New International Version" are trademarks registered in the United States Patent and Trademark Office by Biblica, Inc.®

Scripture quotations marked (NLT) are taken from the Holy Bible, New Living Translation, copyright © 1996, 2004, 2015 by Tyndale House Foundation. Used by permission of Tyndale House Publishers, Carol Stream, Illinois 60188. All rights reserved.

The Daily Grace Co.® exists to equip disciples to know and love God and His Word by creating beautiful, theologically rich, and accessible resources so that God may be glorified and the gospel made known.

Designed in the United States of America and printed in China.

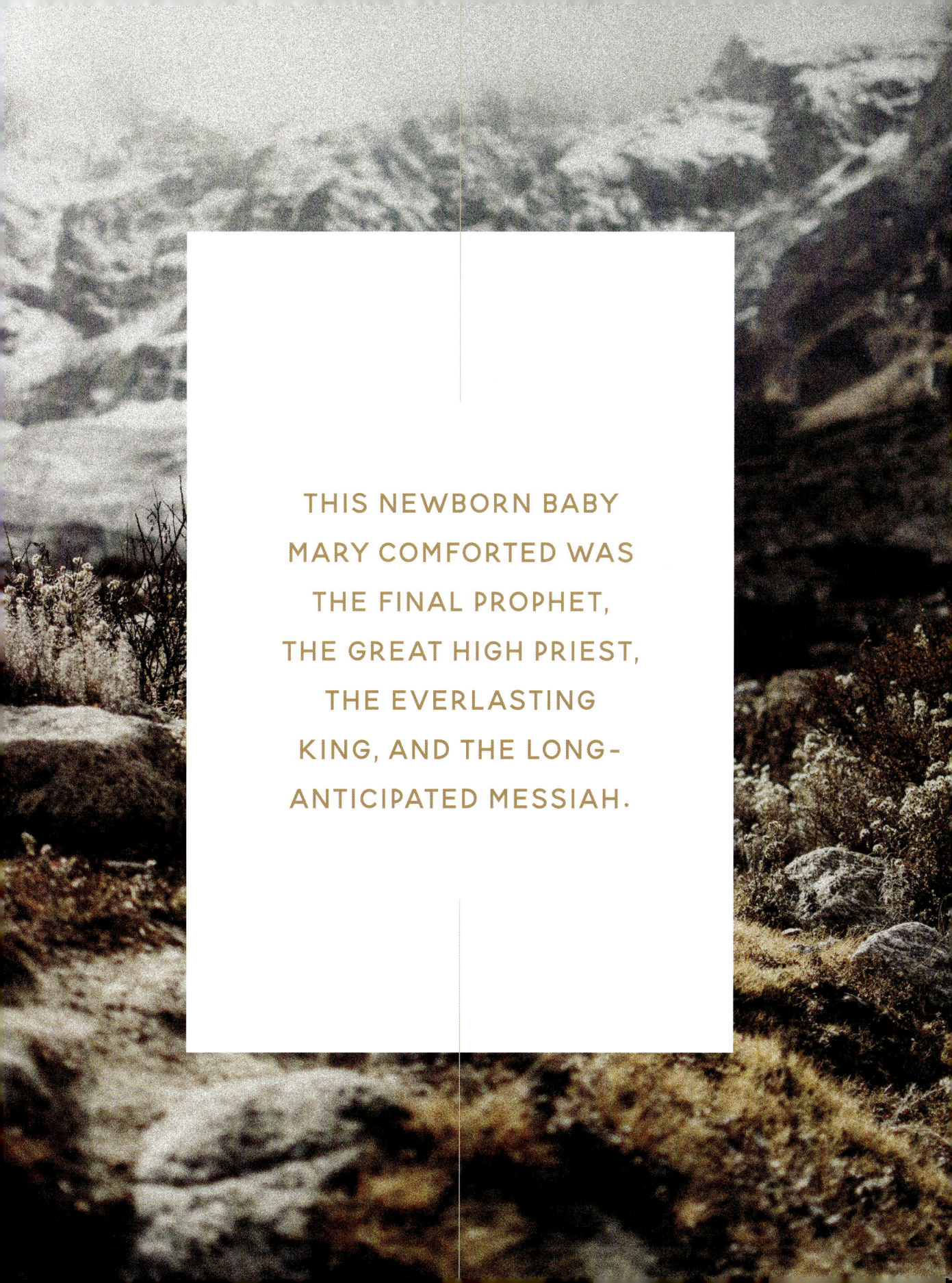

THIS NEWBORN BABY
MARY COMFORTED WAS
THE FINAL PROPHET,
THE GREAT HIGH PRIEST,
THE EVERLASTING
KING, AND THE LONG-
ANTICIPATED MESSIAH.

# Table of Contents

# STUDY SUGGESTIONS

*We believe that the Bible is true, trustworthy, and timeless and that it is vitally important for all believers. These study suggestions are intended to help you more effectively study Scripture as you seek to know and love God through His Word.*

## SUGGESTED STUDY TOOLS

- Bible

- Double-spaced, printed copy of the Scripture passages that this study covers (You can use a website like www.biblegateway.com to copy the text of a passage and print out a double-spaced copy to be able to mark on easily.)

- Journal to write notes or prayers

- Pens, colored pencils, and highlighters

- Dictionary to look up unfamiliar words

## Pray

Begin your study time in prayer. Ask God to reveal Himself to you, help you understand what you are reading, and transform you with His Word (Psalm 119:18).

 ## Read Scripture

Before you read what is written in each day of the study itself, read the assigned passages of Scripture for that day. Use your double-spaced copy to circle, underline, highlight, draw arrows, and mark in any way you would like to help you dig deeper as you work through a passage.

 ## Memorize Scripture

Each week of the study begins with a memory verse. You may want to write the verse down and place it in a place you will see it often. We also recommend spending a few minutes memorizing the verse before you complete each day's study material.

 ## Read Study Content

Read the daily written content provided for the current study day.

 ## Respond

Answer the questions that appear at the end of each study day.

# HOW TO STUDY THE BIBLE

*The inductive method provides tools for deeper and more intentional Bible study. To study the Bible inductively, work through the steps below after reading background information on the book.*

## Observation + Comprehension
**KEY QUESTION: WHAT DOES THE TEXT SAY?**

After reading the daily Scripture in its entirety at least once, begin working with smaller portions of the Scripture. Read a passage of Scripture repetitively, and then mark the following items in the text:

- *Key or repeated words and ideas*
- *Key themes*
- *Transition words (e.g., therefore, but, because, if/then, likewise, etc.)*
- *Lists*
- *Comparisons and contrasts*
- *Commands*
- *Unfamiliar words (look these up in a dictionary)*
- *Questions you have about the text*

## Interpretation
**KEY QUESTION: WHAT DOES THE TEXT MEAN?**

Once you have annotated the text, work through the following steps to help you interpret its meaning:

- *Read the passage in other versions for a better understanding of the text.*
- *Read cross-references to help interpret Scripture with Scripture.*
- *Paraphrase or summarize the passage to check for understanding.*
- *Identify how the text reflects the metanarrative of Scripture, which is the story of creation, fall, redemption, and restoration.*
- *Read trustworthy commentaries if you need further insight into the meaning of the passage.*

# 3 Application

KEY QUESTION: HOW SHOULD THE TRUTH OF THIS PASSAGE CHANGE ME?

Bible study is not merely an intellectual pursuit. The truths about God, ourselves, and the gospel that we discover in Scripture should produce transformation in our hearts and lives. Answer the following questions and prompts as you consider what you have learned in your study:

- *What attributes of God's character are revealed in the passage?*
- *Consider places where the text directly states the character of God, as well as how His character is revealed through His words and actions.*
- *What do I learn about myself in light of who God is?*
- *Consider how you fall short of God's character, how the text reveals your sin nature, and what it says about your new identity in Christ.*
- *How should this truth change me?*
- *A passage of Scripture may contain direct commands telling us what to do or warnings about sins to avoid in order to help us grow in holiness. Other times, our application flows out of seeing ourselves in light of God's character. As we pray and reflect on how God is calling us to change in light of His Word, we should be asking questions like, "How should I pray for God to change my heart?" and "What practical steps can I take toward cultivating habits of holiness?"*

How to Study the Bible    9

# INTRODUCTION

We are so glad you have decided to study *Good News, Great Joy* this Advent season. Our prayer is that this study draws you closer to Jesus and that you will enter Christmas Day with a renewed sense of awe for all our Savior has done.

We know that the Advent season brings with it so many things: joy, decorations, parties, and a general feeling of excitement for what lies ahead. We also know that the best-laid plans can fall by the wayside when the busyness and stress of the holidays set in. That is why we want to use this introduction section to set you up for success as much as we can. Below, we have included some information and tips to help you make the most of this Advent study as you prepare your heart for the celebration of Christ's birth and, ultimately, His second coming.

## ABOUT THIS STUDY

*Good News, Great Joy* examines the different offices of Christ and how He perfectly fulfills the roles of Prophet, Priest, King, and Messiah. This resource begins on the fourth Sunday before Christmas and ends on Christmas Day. The calendar provided on pages 12–13 provides a quick look at which readings you should complete each day to stay on track. We suggest allowing fifteen to thirty minutes to complete each day's devotional content.

Each week begins with an Advent candle lighting and memory verse. If you are new to the Advent candle lighting tradition, it is helpful to know what the candles represent and how often they are lit. There are five Advent candles: hope, peace, joy, love, and the Christ candle. Traditionally, each Sunday, you will light one new Advent candle. This means that on the first Sunday of Advent, you will light the hope candle. On the second Sunday, you will light the hope and peace candles, and on the third Sunday, you will light the hope, peace, and joy candles, and so on and so forth.

In addition to leading you through Advent candle lighting, each week of this study will also examine a different office of Christ. If you are new to studying the offices of Christ, you can learn more on pages 14–15. We hope that by studying and understanding how Christ is the fulfillment of each of these roles, you will grow closer to Him and find a new love and appreciation for all that Christ has done for you.

## BEFORE YOU BEGIN

As we mentioned previously, we know that the best-laid plans can often go awry during the busy Christmas season. However, we truly believe that the best way to celebrate Christmas is by setting your focus on the One this holiday is all about. Therefore, we recommend taking a look at your calendar and planning out when you will complete each study day. It also may help to find a friend or family member to work through this study with to keep you accountable.

Finally, we pray this resource keeps Christ at the center of it all this holiday season. May this study bring you great delight in seeing God's goodness and grace displayed toward us through sending His Son, and may your eyes and heart be opened anew to the good news of the gospel.

# 2023 ADVENT STUDY
## CALENDAR

| SUNDAY | MONDAY | TUESDAY |
|---|---|---|
| **WEEK 1: JESUS IS THE PERFECT PROPHET WHO FULFILLS EVERY PROPHECY AND BRINGS US HOPE.** | | |
| **3** CANDLE LIGHTING: HOPE<br><br>MEMORY VERSE: JOHN 1:5 | **4** WHAT IS THE ROLE OF A PROPHET? | **5** DIFFERENT TIMES AND IN DIFFERENT WAYS |
| **WEEK 2: JESUS IS OUR GREAT HIGH PRIEST WHO GIVES US PEACE.** | | |
| **10** CANDLE LIGHTING: PEACE<br><br>MEMORY VERSE: ISAIAH 1:18B | **11** WHAT IS THE ROLE OF A PRIEST? | **12** OUR NEED FOR A PRIEST |
| **WEEK 3: JESUS IS THE KING OF KINGS WHO FILLS US WITH JOY.** | | |
| **17** CANDLE LIGHTING: JOY<br><br>MEMORY VERSE: PSALM 100:4 | **18** WHAT IS THE ROLE OF A KING? | **19** THE REJECTION OF THE KING |
| **CHRISTMAS: JESUS CHRIST IS THE MESSIAH WHO LOVES US SO MUCH HE CAME TO SAVE US.** | | |
| **24** CANDLE LIGHTING: LOVE<br><br>MEMORY VERSE: ISAIAH 9:6<br><br>WHO IS THE MESSIAH? | **25** CANDLE LIGHTING: CHRIST CANDLE<br><br>JESUS: THE MESSIAH IS HERE! | |

| WEDNESDAY | THURSDAY | FRIDAY | S |
|---|---|---|---|

| 6 | 7 | 8 | APPLICATION |
|---|---|---|---|
| THE ANTICIPATED PROPHET | JESUS: THE PERFECT REVELATION | JESUS: THE FULFILLMENT OF PROPHECY | |

| 13 | 14 | 15 | APPLICATION |
|---|---|---|---|
| THE ANTICIPATED PRIEST | JESUS: THE GREAT HIGH PRIEST | JESUS: OUR PRIEST | |

| 20 | 21 | 22 | APPLICATION |
|---|---|---|---|
| THE ANTICIPATED KING | JESUS: THE KING OF KINGS | JESUS: THE KINGDOM OF CHRIST | |

# INTRODUCTION

## TO THE OFFICES OF CHRIST

What do you think of when you consider a person of authority? Maybe you think of the president of a country, the CEO of a company, or the chairman of a board. A position of authority can be referred to as an office. For example, the Executive Office of the President is not a large working space with a desk and computer. Instead, it refers to a group of people who receive authority to work alongside the President of the United States in matters that affect the country. But did you know that Jesus is considered to have different offices? While Scripture does not use the language of "office" specifically, based on what we see and learn about Jesus from the Bible, there are three offices that Jesus bears: Prophet, Priest, and King. While this study will dive more deeply into each of these offices, it is helpful to first have a general understanding of what each of these offices means.

**PROPHET**    Jesus is the true and better Prophet. Though God used prophets
    in the Old Testament to speak God's words to His people, Jesus is the very Word of God (John 1). Jesus came to earth and took on flesh to share God's truth and wisdom with people and provide eternal life through the words He taught and by His death and resurrection.

**PRIEST**    Jesus is our Great High Priest (Hebrews 4:14) who reconciled
    mankind to God through His own sacrifice on the cross. While the priests in the Old Testament made offerings on behalf of God's people, Jesus offered Himself as a sacrifice on our behalf, providing permanent forgiveness for our sin.

**KING**  The Old Testament is full of earthly kings who ruled over Israel and other nations. But all of these kings fall short in light of Jesus, who is the one true King. Jesus is King because He rules and reigns over all things. Christ inaugurated God's kingdom through His life, death, resurrection, and ascension. And through Jesus, we are able to be part of the kingdom of God.

**MESSIAH**  Connected to all three of these offices is the title of Messiah. While Messiah is not considered an official office, the truth that Jesus is the Messiah enhances our understanding of who Jesus is. Messiah means "Anointed One," and throughout Scripture, the name Messiah refers to the promised Savior who would rescue and deliver God's people from their sins. Advent is the season in which we remember and rejoice over the Messiah, Jesus, who came to save us and set us free.

Advent is a time of anticipation, a season of waiting as we count down the days until Christmas. In this season, we place ourselves in the shoes of the Israelites, who anticipated the promised Messiah who would redeem people from their sins, reconcile people to God, and restore God's kingdom. We ready ourselves for Christmas, not only by setting up our trees and wrapping presents but by preparing our hearts through God's Word. This study will help you do just that. Through this study, you will grow deeper in your understanding of the baby born in Bethlehem: Jesus, who is our Prophet, Priest, King, and Messiah. You will learn how Jesus perfectly fulfills each of these offices and how He is faithful to redeem, reconcile, and restore.

As you grow in your understanding of who Jesus is, so will your excitement during the season of Advent grow, for the celebrated baby at Christmas has done more than we could ever imagine. He is our Prophet, Priest, King, and Messiah, who cleanses our hearts, unites us to the Father, and grants us a permanent place in God's kingdom. Though presents sit ready to be unwrapped under our Christmas trees, Jesus is the greatest gift we could ever receive.

# Prophet

JESUS IS THE PERFECT PROPHET
WHO FULFILLS EVERY PROPHECY
AND BRINGS US HOPE.

Candle Lighting

# Hope

1 · 1

Today, we will light the hope candle and remember that
Jesus is our hope—yesterday, today, and forever.

FATHER,

As we light this first candle of Advent, we thank You for the hope
You brought to the world over two thousand years ago. Thank
You for sending Your Son as the fulfillment of a promise You
made to Your people thousands of years ago. We praise You
that, through Jesus, our sins have been washed away and that
we can live with hope for a day when tears will flow no more.

WE PRAY THIS IN YOUR SON'S PRECIOUS NAME,

AMEN

# Memory
# Verse

| . |

That light shines in the
darkness, and yet the darkness
did not overcome it.

JOHN 1:5

God desires to speak
to His people.

# What Is the Role of a Prophet?

READ DEUTERONOMY 13:1 – 5, DEUTERONOMY 18:9 – 22

We know that wise men, shepherds, and angels are part of the Christmas story, but did you know that prophets are also part of the Christmas story? While we do not see prophets show up in the actual story of Christ's birth, the prophets in the Bible are intricately tied to the baby born in Bethlehem. Their messages and ministries were intentionally used by God to point to the child to come, the child who would be the fulfillment of God's promises. So before we get to that starry night in Bethlehem, before we get to the angel's chorus and the shepherd's wonder, and before we get to the cries of a newborn in a manger, let us go backward in history and meet these prophets who impact the Advent narrative.

In the Bible, a prophet's main role was to be a mouthpiece for God. They would speak on behalf of God by relaying God's Word to the people. Prophets always spoke the words of the Lord and derived their authority from God alone. Every genuine prophet in Scripture had a moment in which God came directly to him and gave that prophet the authority to speak for Him. For instance, in Jeremiah 1:9–10, the prophet Jeremiah recounts how God gave him the authority to speak for Him when he wrote:

Then the Lord reached out his hand, touched my mouth, and told me: I have now filled your mouth with my words. See, I have appointed you today over nations and kingdoms to uproot and tear down, to destroy and demolish, to build and plant.

These verses reveal how God put His words inside Jeremiah to speak and how God appointed him specifically to be a prophet for the people of Israel.

While prophets did speak to future events and foretold God's plans of judgment or restoration, prophets were primarily used by God to lead the Israelites in their faithfulness to Him. Second Chronicles 24:19 tells us how God "sent them prophets to bring them back to the Lord; they admonished them, but the people would not listen." Prophets would use the messages God gave them to encourage the people to remember the holiness of the Lord, call them to repent from their sins, and challenge them to remain obedient to God's covenant. Often, prophets placed themselves in difficult situations and faced persecution for the messages they delivered to God's people. Nevertheless, God protected the prophets He sent out and used them to declare His promises and admonishments.

---

## God protected the prophets He sent out and used them to declare His promises and admonishments.

---

You may be wondering, *Why were there prophets in Scripture if God could speak directly to man?* In Exodus 20:18–21, the Israelites witnessed the effects of God's glory from afar as He met with Moses atop Mount Sinai. When they saw the thunder, lightning, and smoke on the mountain that accompanied God's presence, the people were afraid. So, in Exodus 20:18–21, the Israelites asked Moses to meet with God on their behalf and to tell them God's words instead of having God speak to them directly. Deuteronomy 18:16 references this past situation as one reason why God gave and sent prophets to His people.

Scripture also tells us of false prophets who were not genuine prophets of God. These prophets were self-appointed rather than appointed by God and therefore spoke with their own authority rather than the authority of the Lord. These false prophets often used certain practices to determine and declare the truth. They would sometimes use forms of divination like fortune telling, spells, or searching the entrails of animals to discover messages from God (Deuteronomy 18:9–10). A defining factor of a false prophet would be someone who leads people away in their worship of God rather than one who spurs them on in their worship. God warns against these kinds of people in Deuteronomy 13:1–3 and commands His people not to listen to prophets who encourage them to follow and worship other gods.

Another characteristic of a false prophet would be the failure to consistently provide predictions that came true. God tells His people in Deuteronomy 18:20–22 how they can recognize a message that is not from Him: if the messenger speaks in God's name, but their message does not come true. If this happens, they have made presumptions rather than speaking something directly from the Lord.

The establishment of prophets in Scripture reveals how God desires to speak to His people. While the Israelites resisted having God speak to them directly, God still made it possible for His people to hear His words through the prophets. God's words to the prophets also reveal intimacy as God chose them to hear and relay His words. Prophecy in the Bible shows us how God does not remain at a distance but comes near to His people in intimate ways. God's use of prophets in Scripture also attests to His desire to give wisdom and direction to His people. It was kind of the Lord to raise up prophets to help guide and lead His people in their faithfulness to Him. God is also gracious to give warnings to His people and promises of hope and restoration through the prophets.

And while prophets in the Old Testament relayed God's words, there was a time coming when God would speak to His people directly. One day, in the little town of Bethlehem, the Word of God would be born as a baby, and the people would receive God's revelation face to face.

# QUESTIONS

**1**  How did today's study deepen your understanding of prophets?

QUESTIONS CONTINUE ▶

**2** Why do you think there were (and still are) people who claim to have a message from God when they really do not?

**3** Why is it important to listen to and obey the Word of God? How can you practically listen to and obey God's Word?

**Notes**

*God's grace shines even in the darkness of judgment.*

# Different Times and in Different Ways

On the night Jesus was born, something spectacular happened. While humble shepherds attended to their flocks, an angel suddenly appeared to them, proclaiming "good news of great joy that will be for all the people" (Luke 2:10). This news would change everything, and the shepherds accepted the angel's message with wonder and delight. The response of these shepherds contrasts greatly with the response of God's people to His messengers in the Old Testament. God's prophets often proclaimed messages that seemed like anything but "good news of great joy." But the words of the prophets in the Old Testament mattered just as much as the words of the heavenly herald in the Christmas story.

Hebrews 1:1 tells us that "long ago God spoke to the ancestors by the prophets at different times and in different ways." Each Old Testament prophet served a specific purpose in the history of God's people, the Israelites. The first time the word "prophet" appears in Scripture is in Genesis 20:7 when God refers to Abraham as a prophet. The next well-known prophet to come after Abraham was Moses. While God used Abraham to establish the nation of Israel, it was Moses whom God used to lead Israel to the Promised Land that God promised to Abraham. Although Abraham was faithful to the Lord, Deuteronomy 34:10 states how no prophet arose in Israel who was like Moses because God knew Moses face to face. Moses had an intimate relationship with the Lord, and even though he failed in many ways, he was God's instrument to guide the people in their faithfulness to the Lord.

Unfortunately, the further we journey through the Old Testament, the greater God's people grew in their wickedness. They rebelled against the Lord and desired to take matters into their own hands rather than submit themselves to God. One primary example of Israel's rebellion was when Israel demanded to have a king like their surrounding nations (1 Samuel 8). God used a prophet by the name of Samuel to speak to the people of Israel during this time. It was Samuel's task to find the king whom God chose to lead the Israelites and to speak to the king on God's behalf. Just like the prophets before him, Samuel sought to encourage Israel's faithfulness to God as their ultimate King, even though they had now chosen someone to rule over them. After the first king of Israel failed, Samuel found and anointed David, whom God specifically chose to lead the Israelites.

David was far from a perfect king, but by God's grace and faithfulness, the nation of Israel flourished under his reign. They were a united people who were encouraged by David to worship and obey the Lord. Sadly, this all changed when David died. When David's son, Solomon, took the throne, it seemed as if Solomon would follow in his father's footsteps. But Solomon eventually turned his heart away from the Lord, influencing the hearts of God's people to turn away as well.

Israel's situation only worsened as Solomon's son, Rehoboam, took the throne, and Rehoboam's actions caused the kingdom of Israel to split. Now, Israel was a divided kingdom. The broken nation reflected the brokenness of the hearts of God's people, who no longer desired to worship and obey the Lord.

But God is a gracious God, and He pursues His people no matter the condition of their hearts. Out of His grace, God continued to provide prophets to encourage repentance and renewed worship of the Lord. In the initial stages of the divided kingdom, God appointed the prophets Elijah and Elisha. Elijah, in particular, is considered one of the most important prophets in Israel's history, and he is known to have greatly impacted Israel's returned worship of God. Both Elijah and Elisha were also given power by God to do miraculous works. The words and works of these prophets revealed the glory of God, encouraging the Israelites to turn from idols who paled in comparison to the one true God.

And while there were moments of returned worship and repentance under Elijah and Elisha's influence, the Israelites would always resume their rebellious ways and worship of other gods. The majority of kings who took the throne over the two kingdoms were wicked, and God's people continued to do what was evil in God's sight. Yet God did not give up on His people, even though they had been unfaithful to Him. God continued to send prophet after prophet to both kingdoms to encourage the kings to obey the Lord and the people to repent of their sin. We receive detailed accounts of these prophecies in the prophetic books of Scripture, categorized as the Major and Minor Prophets.

The Major and Minor Prophets are often perceived as being all about "doom and gloom." These books contain prophecies of judgment upon Israel and surrounding nations. And because of Israel's constant unrepentance, even with the prophets' warnings, these prophecies came true as God's people were overcome by other nations and taken into exile. God's words of judgment were just because of the seriousness of Israel's sin and the wickedness of their hearts. Thankfully, God did not only speak judgment upon His people. God's grace shines even in the darkness of judgment, for God promised to restore and redeem His people. God used both the Major and Minor Prophets to declare His promised purposes to save His people and bring them to Himself.

The Old Testament prophets teach us about God's jealousy for His people, the seriousness of our sin, and God's faithfulness to redeem and restore, even though His people rebel against Him. Yet the failure of God's people to listen to the prophets and maintain faithfulness to the Lord sets the stage for Jesus, the one true Prophet who will succeed in guiding people to obey and worship the Lord (Hebrews 1:1–4). He will proclaim good news of great joy that will establish genuine repentance and true heart change.

# QUESTIONS

**1** What does Israel's rebellion reveal about the human heart?

QUESTIONS CONTINUE ▶

**2** How is God's grace evident through the words of the prophets?

**3** How does the gospel encourage our repentance and worship of God?

**Notes**

# TIMELINE OF MAJOR AND MINOR
# PROPHETS

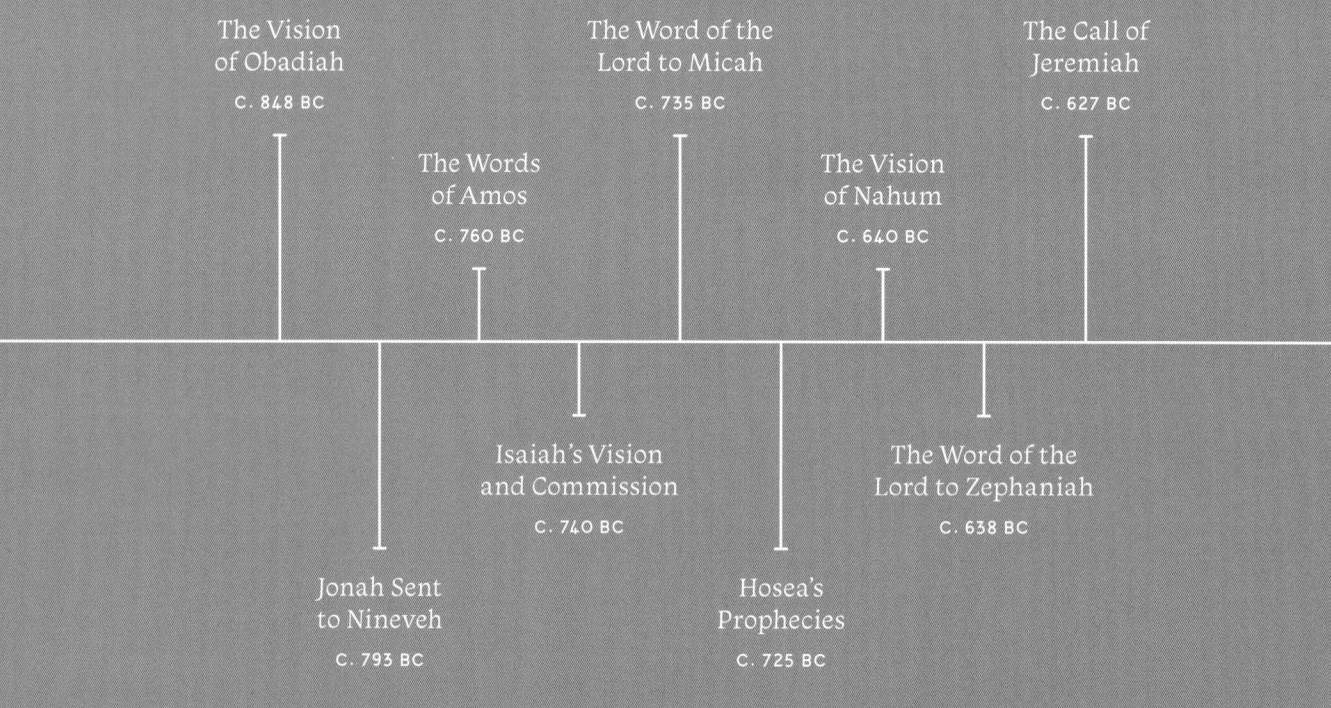

The Vision
of Obadiah

C. 848 BC

The Words
of Amos

C. 760 BC

The Word of the
Lord to Micah

C. 735 BC

The Vision
of Nahum

C. 640 BC

The Call of
Jeremiah

C. 627 BC

Jonah Sent
to Nineveh

C. 793 BC

Isaiah's Vision
and Commission

C. 740 BC

Hosea's
Prophecies

C. 725 BC

The Word of the
Lord to Zephaniah

C. 638 BC

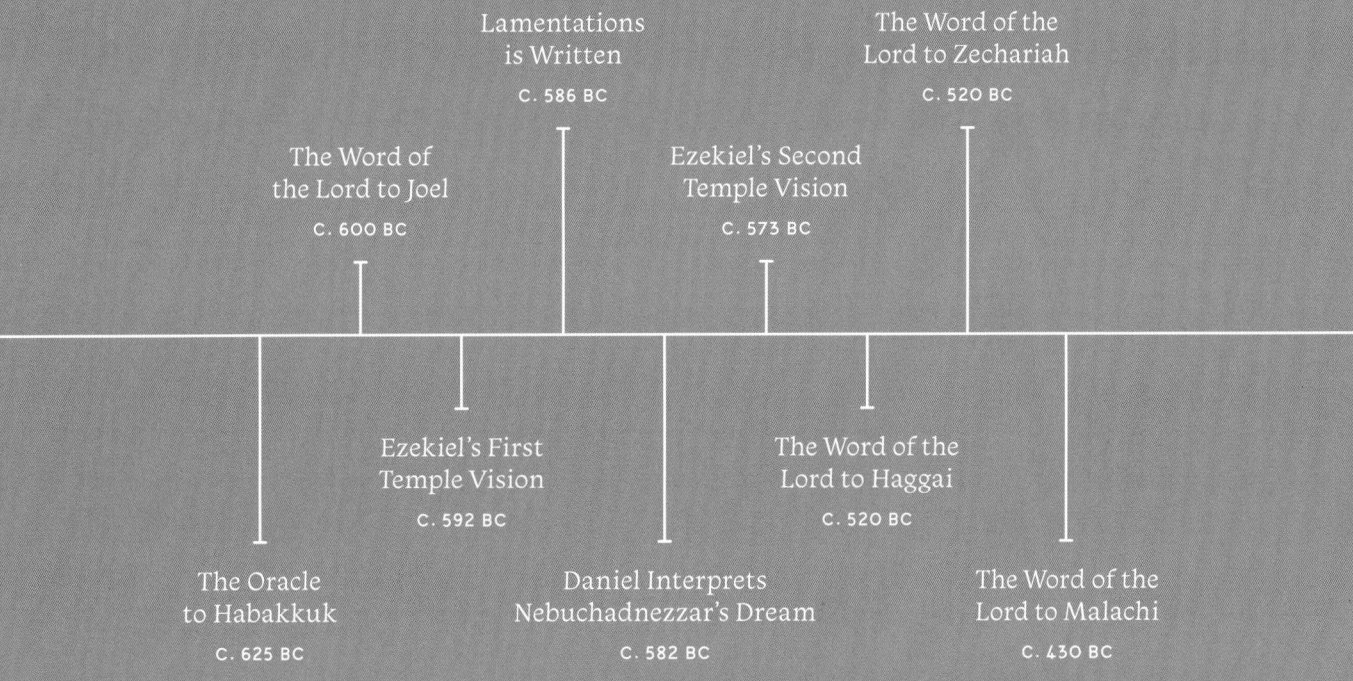

Lamentations
is Written

C. 586 BC

The Word of the
Lord to Zechariah

C. 520 BC

The Word of
the Lord to Joel

C. 600 BC

Ezekiel's Second
Temple Vision

C. 573 BC

Ezekiel's First
Temple Vision

C. 592 BC

The Word of the
Lord to Haggai

C. 520 BC

The Oracle
to Habakkuk

C. 625 BC

Daniel Interprets
Nebuchadnezzar's Dream

C. 582 BC

The Word of the
Lord to Malachi

C. 430 BC

# PROPHETS

Throughout Israel's history, many prophets spoke the word of the Lord to His people. The information below briefly highlights each prophet's ministry. It is important to note that the kingdom of Israel split into two in c. 931 BC (1 Kings 12). The northern kingdom was called Israel, and the southern kingdom was called Judah. Because of this, we have identified which kingdom each prophet spoke to, noting that some prophesied to both kingdoms and some prophesied to the surrounding nations. As you read about both the Major and Minor Prophets, remember that all of these prophets ultimately point to our need for a true and better Prophet, Jesus Christ, whom we celebrate at Christmas.

## MAJOR PROPHETS

### Isaiah

**Prophesied to:** Judah

**Main message:** God's judgment of Judah because of the Israelites' unfaithfulness; God's promises of restoration, especially through a promised Messiah

**Key themes:**
- God's just judgment
- The promised Messiah
- God's grace
- God's gift of restoration

### Jeremiah

**Prophesied to:** Judah

**Main message:** Judah's sinfulness and their need for repentance, as well as God's promises of restoration

**Key themes:**
- God's just judgment
- God's gift of restoration
- The new covenant

## Lamentations

*Prophesied to:* Judah

*Main message:* Grief over Judah's sins and judgment

*Key themes:*
- Trust in God's sovereignty
- Lament
- Hope in God's restoration

## Ezekiel

*Prophesied to:* Judah

*Main message:* Warning of God's judgment against Judah and God's promises to restore Judah and Jerusalem

*Key themes:*
- God's just judgment
- God's gift of restoration
- Worship restored

## Daniel

*Prophesied to:* Judah and surrounding kingdoms

*Main message:* God's plan to save and restore His people from all oppressors

*Key themes:*
- God's sovereignty and faithfulness
- God's just retribution
- God's eternal and supreme kingdom

## Hosea

*Prophesied to:* Israel

*Main message:* The coming Assyrian exile and the need for repentance

*Key themes:*
- God's covenantal love
- God's just judgment
- God's gift of restoration

## Joel

*Prophesied to:* Israel

*Main message:* God's judgment through the Day of the Lord, the need for repentance, and God's promises of restoration

*Key themes:*
- God's just judgment
- God's gift of restoration
- The gift of the Spirit

## Amos

*Prophesied to:* Israel

*Main message:* God's judgment by Assyrian exile, the need for repentance, and God's promises of restoration

*Key themes:*
- God's heart for justice
- God's gift of restoration

## Obadiah

*Prophesied to:* Israel and Judah

*Main message:* God's judgment against Edom and Israel's promised restoration

*Key themes:*
- God's sovereignty
- God's heart for justice and just retribution
- God's gift of restoration

## Jonah

*Prophesied to:* Nineveh

*Main message:* God's warning of judgment if Nineveh does not repent, reflecting Israel's need for repentance

*Key themes:*
- God's grace and compassion
- Repentance

## Micah

*Prophesied to:* Israel and Judah

*Main message:* God's judgment upon Israel but also God's restoration

*Key themes:*
- The promised Deliverer
- God's promised deliverance
- Retribution for injustice

## Nahum

**Prophesied to:** Nineveh

**Main message:** God's judgment upon Nineveh for not repenting

**Key themes:**
- God's just judgment
- God's gift of restoration

## Habakkuk

**Prophesied to:** Judah

**Main message:** God's judgment upon Babylon

**Key themes:**
- God's justice
- God's sovereignty to use bad for good

## Zephaniah

**Prophesied to:** Judah

**Main message:** Judgment for both Judah and surrounding nations but also God's promise of restoration

**Key themes:**
- God's just judgment
- God's gift of restoration

## Haggai

**Prophesied to:** Judah

**Main message:** The initiation of the reconstruction of the temple

**Key themes:**
- God's faithfulness
- Restored worship

## Zechariah

**Prophesied to:** Judah

**Main message:** Judah's sin and the need for repentance, as well as God's promises of restoration

**Key themes:**
- The promised Messiah
- God's sovereignty
- Repentance

## Malachi

**Prophesied to:** Israel

**Main message:** Israel's need to repent and the Day of the Lord

**Key themes:**
- A promised Deliverer
- God's just judgment
- God's desire for worship and faithfulness

Only Jesus can Truly turn our hearts to the Lord.

# The Anticipated Prophet

**READ DEUTERONOMY 18:15 – 18, LUKE 1:11 – 17**

We help our kids count down the days until Christmas with Advent calendars full of chocolate. We look forward to gathering with friends and family we do not often see throughout the year on Christmas Day. We grow excited to open that one special present we have asked to receive. Anticipation breeds delight, especially when we are waiting for something that brings us joy. The Israelites knew what it was like to wait with anticipation. Nestled between words about true prophets in the Old Testament, we find a promise of a Prophet to come. And while the Israelites might not have anticipated Him when they were rebellious and wayward, they were likely anticipating a prophet as they went hundreds of years without hearing from God.

In Deuteronomy 18:15–18, Moses shares God's promise to raise up a prophet. Most Bible interpreters believe that with this promise, God was speaking about the line of prophets who would arise after Moses died. God promised that these prophets would speak His words and come from among His people. Just like Moses, God promised that these future prophets would receive God's words in their mouths and tell all that God commanded them to say. And as we saw in our study yesterday, God did indeed raise up prophets for the people of Israel after Moses's death. Yet the people did not heed God's command in Deuteronomy 18:15 that they must listen to these prophets. While some did listen to the prophets God sent and some repentance did occur, the nation of Israel, on the whole, continued to do what was wrong in God's eyes.

But the Israelites were then impacted greatly by something they probably never expected: God stopped sending prophets, and the people stopped receiving the word of the Lord. After the Israelites were brought out of exile and restored to their land, God did not speak for approximately four hundred years. The last prophet recorded in Scripture is the prophet Malachi, and the book of Malachi finishes with these words: "Look, I am going to send you the prophet Elijah before the great and terrible day of the Lord comes. And he will turn the hearts of fathers to their children and the hearts of children to their fathers. Otherwise, I will come and strike the land with a curse" (Malachi 4:5–6). With these final words, prophecy ceased for a time. Because of the sudden cessation of prophecy, Bible interpreters believe that the Israelites began to view Deuteronomy 18:15–18 as a prophecy about one particular person who would come. And Malachi 4:5–6 seems to confirm this.

During the four hundred years of silence, the Israelites were likely in a time of anticipation. As the years went by and God still had not provided His promised Prophet, the Israelites probably thought, *When will this promised Prophet come? Will God speak to us again?* It is possible that because of Malachi 4:5–6, people expected the Prophet Elijah to come again. But God's mention of Elijah is best understood as a description of the person coming rather than Elijah returning

himself. This Prophet would be like Elijah and would carry on Elijah's work by turning the hearts of God's people to the Lord.

Though the Israelites could not have predicted it then, we now know that this Prophet did come, and He was preceded by another who was sent to prepare the way for Him (Luke 3:4). In Luke 1:11–17, we read how the angel Gabriel appeared to a man named Zechariah. Gabriel told Zechariah how his wife would bear a son who would have an incredible destiny. This boy would be given God's Spirit and would turn many hearts to the Lord. Gabriel's words are very similar to those in Malachi 4:5–6, especially with the mention of Elijah (Malachi 4:5, Luke 1:17). Just as Zechariah might have thought, we can find ourselves wondering, *Is this the promised Prophet?* Later on in Luke 1, Zechariah prophesies this about his son, "And you, child, will be called a prophet of the Most High, for you will go before the Lord to prepare his ways" (Luke 1:76).

While Zechariah's son, John the Baptist, would be a prophet of the Most High, he would not be *the* Prophet God promised. Instead, John the Baptist would be a herald for the promised Prophet to come — the One who would be not only a prophet but also the Lord, the Messiah, God in the flesh. This promised Prophet is Jesus, who would go on to turn hearts to the Lord through an agonizing death on the cross. But would the people heed God's words to listen to Jesus, the true promised Prophet of God?

We see the answer to that question in John 7:40, when some people saw the miraculous works Jesus performed and said, "This truly is the Prophet" (John 7:40). However, while some people recognized Jesus as God's prophet and listened to His words, others rejected Him

(John 7:41). After so many years of anticipation, God's people did not welcome Jesus as God's true promised Prophet. This rejection would be like us slamming the door in the face of the person we had been excited to see on Christmas Day or opening a gift we had desired, only to then toss it aside in disgust.

However, even with this rejection, Jesus remained faithful to teaching God's words. But unlike the prophets before Him, Jesus did what those prophets could not do by saving God's people from their sin. While the prophets helped encourage obedience and worship, only Jesus can truly turn our hearts to the Lord and keep them there by His grace. This Advent season, we have a choice to make. Will we reject the baby in the manger who died for us, or will we receive Him? As we count down the days until Christmas, may our hearts be soft and open to Jesus because unlike the Israelites, this season of anticipation is not a time of silence but celebration. Jesus has come, and He now draws all His children to Himself, teaching us to listen to Him and grow in obedience as He transforms our hearts.

## QUESTIONS

**1** How would you feel as an Israelite during the four hundred years of silence?

QUESTIONS CONTINUE ▶

**2**    Why does it matter that God remained faithful to provide the promised Prophet?

**3**    Why did the people reject Jesus, even though He was the anticipated Prophet?

# Notes

*God speaks to us through His Son.*

# Jesus: The Perfect Revelation

**READ HEBREWS 1:1–2, JOHN 1:1, JOHN 14:9**

The Israelites lived without a prophet's words for four hundred years. During these years, the Israelites eventually came under Roman rule. They had returned to their land from exile, but they faced heavy taxation and oppression from the Roman government. As such, the Israelites once again found themselves in a place of hardship. Throughout this time, there was no word from God, no prophet giving the people encouragement and instruction from the Lord. But this all changed one night in Bethlehem. That night, the Word of God broke through the silence, and heaven met earth like never before. The anticipated Prophet came, yet He was completely different from what people expected. The Word of God was a baby boy born in a manger.

Yet this child was unlike those who came before Him. While He grew up and began sharing God's words with the people, He claimed an authority that the prophets of old did not possess. Yes, this man's authority to proclaim God's words came from God, but He also claimed to share equality with the One who provided Him authority. This was because Jesus — the true Prophet, God's promised Prophet — is God in the flesh.

John 1:14 tells us, "The Word became flesh and dwelt among us. We observed his glory, the glory as the one and only Son from the Father, full of grace and truth." The Word is Jesus Christ, who was with God in the beginning and shares God's nature. It was God's plan from the start to send a Prophet who would be set apart from the rest who came before Him. Jesus is distinct from the prophets because Jesus did not only speak God's words—He is the Word of God, the revelation of God in human form. While those before Him revealed God's wisdom and instruction, Jesus is the perfect revelation. Only Jesus can communicate God's truth and wisdom perfectly because He is God.

Jesus revealed the Father in a way the prophets could not because He enabled mankind to be face-to-face with God Himself. Those who saw Jesus speak heard God's words from the very lips of God. This is why Jesus tells His disciples in John 14:9 that those who see Him have seen the Father. To see, hear, and know Jesus is to see, hear, and know God. However, Jesus is also distinct from the prophets because He did not only speak on behalf of God. He called people to follow Him and experience new life through Him.

Jesus declares in John 14:6 that He is the only way to God. Jesus reveals the Father to humanity, but He also reveals the way to know the Father—through Him. Those who believe in Jesus and follow Him receive a relationship with God and eternal life. Through Christ, we receive new hearts and a new way of life that is dedicated to the Lord. Therefore, Jesus is the answer for our wayward hearts and misaligned worship.

While the past prophets encouraged God's people to follow God and His law, they were still sinful humans themselves. Yet Jesus did not waver in His obedience to God. He remained faithful to the Lord and did what God's people could not by meeting all the requirements of God's law. Jesus lived the perfect life that we could never live and died the death that we deserve. But through His death and resurrection, those who trust and believe in Jesus receive the ability to be faithful to the Lord. With our hearts cleansed from sin and with the help of the Holy Spirit, we are enabled to walk in the newness of life that Christ gives us.

---

## God's revelation remained consistent throughout time and culminated in Jesus Christ.

---

Each one of us is separated from God because of our sin. Desperately though we may try, we cannot do anything on our own to bridge the chasm between us and God that sin has created. But this is why God gave us Jesus. The prophets of old were only a shadow of the true Prophet, Jesus, who unites us to the Father. The cross of Christ bridges the gap between us and God. Through the grace of Christ, we are able to run to the open arms of the Father and live as the people God created us to be. Sin kept us from obeying and worshiping the Lord as we should, but the new hearts we receive from Christ turn us away from our sinful pursuits to follow the Lord. Even when we stray in our faithfulness to the Lord, the grace of Christ brings us back, and the Spirit enables us to keep pursuing the Lord.

This Advent, consider God's incredible grace to send His people His Word. Consider God's faithfulness to provide salvation even when it seemed like He was silent. God's revelation remained consistent throughout time and culminated in Jesus Christ. Even in those years of silence, God remained faithful to bring His people to Himself. Yet He did not send a mere man to do this, but He sent His own Son.

Whatever you may be experiencing this Advent season, do not allow those situations and emotions to keep you from marveling at Jesus Christ. Do not lose sight of the new life that Jesus Christ has given you or offers you. In the past, God spoke through the prophets, but now, He has spoken to us through His Son. And when we listen to Jesus and follow Him, our lives are transformed. The baby born in Bethlehem changed everything, so let us respond to Him with adoration and praise.

# QUESTIONS

**1** How was Jesus distinct from the prophets before Him? Why is Jesus more than a prophet?

QUESTIONS CONTINUE ▶

**2** Read Mark 8:34–38. How are our lives changed by following Christ? Why is the cost to follow Christ worth it?

**3** How does the life that Jesus gives you motivate your obedience to God?

**Notes**

God is a God of
promises, and He will
always fulfill His promises.

# Jesus: The Fulfillment of Prophecy

**READ LUKE 24:25 – 27, 1 PETER 1:10 – 12**

The day after Christmas can feel pretty disheartening. The excitement of Christmas fades once the day has passed. The presents have all been unwrapped, the Christmas tree is ready to be taken down, and a regular routine begins again. We might combat these feelings of disappointment by looking ahead to the next Christmas. Children may get started on their Christmas lists for next year early, and parents may feel content when taking down the tree, knowing that the day will come for it to be decorated again. Hope is fueled by looking ahead. Whether it be Christmas Day or another anticipated event, our hope grows by looking ahead to what we know will happen.

Many prophecies in the Old Testament involved looking ahead. God, in His faithfulness, partially fulfilled His promises for Israel—such as releasing them from exile and returning them to their land—but there was still something to hope for. Israel was still under foreign rule, the temple was not what it used to be, and the promised Messiah had not come. Yet the Israelites could find hope as they read the prophecies God gave them and looked ahead to their fulfillment.

Though they were unrepentant and wayward, God provided glimpses of grace through prophecies. God gave the prophets prophecies of restoration, such as in Ezekiel 34:27b, which says, "They will know that I am the Lord when I break the bars of their yoke and rescue them from the power of those who enslave them." God declared prophecies of forgiveness, such as in Isaiah 1:18, which says, "'Come, let's settle this,' says the Lord. 'Though your sins are scarlet, they will be as white as snow; though they are crimson red, they will be like wool.'" God also provided prophecies of a new covenant that He would establish with His people (Jeremiah 31), and God gave prophecy after prophecy of the chosen Messiah, who would be God's agent of salvation and restoration (Isaiah 9:6, Jeremiah 33:14–15).

While many of the prophecies God gave the Israelites contained warnings and punishment, God remained faithful to always provide prophecies that fostered hope. Even before God used prophets, He spoke promises to His people, forming covenants with them that promised a future of abundance, freedom, and peace. God's words of promise even trace back to the garden of Eden, where God Himself first declared how the Messiah would defeat Satan (Genesis 3:15). God is a God of promises, and He will always fulfill His promises.

First Peter 1:10–12 tells us how the prophets in the Old Testament searched through past and current prophecies to determine when and how the Messiah would come. These verses show how the Holy Spirit foretold what the Messiah would accomplish and also how He would suffer. Therefore, the prophets were given a general understanding of the Messiah, and they looked ahead to His coming. Through prophets like Isaiah, we are able to read prophecies of the birth, life, and death of Jesus that the Holy Spirit gave to the prophets. But unlike the prophets, we have witnessed these prophecies fulfilled.

While many prophecies were partially fulfilled in Israel's history, all of the prophecies in the Old Testament ultimately point us toward Jesus and are fulfilled in Him. We can see this for ourselves in the Christmas stories we often read during Advent. The Gospel of Matthew repeatedly shows how certain events fulfilled prophecies in Scripture. The virgin birth and Jesus being born in Bethlehem, for example, are but two of these many fulfillments (Matthew 1:22–23, Matthew 2:5–6).

But it would be Jesus's death on the cross and His resurrection from the dead that would ultimately fulfill God's promises. God's promises of redemption, salvation, forgiveness, and restoration all find their fulfillment in Jesus Christ. Through Jesus's death and resurrection, those who repent and believe in Him are released from their bondage to sin, saved from the punishment of their sin, forgiven of all of their sins, and restored in their relationship with God. Therefore, Jesus is not only the true and better Prophet but the fulfillment of every prophecy in Scripture.

Second Corinthians 1:20 tells us how "every one of God's promises is 'Yes' in him." God has declared His great faithfulness by fulfilling His promises through Christ, even the covenantal promises spoken to Abraham, Issac, and David. However, though many of God's promises have been fulfilled through Christ, we still await the day when God's promises of complete redemption and restoration will be fulfilled when Jesus returns to make all things new. Like the prophets and the Israelites, we look ahead to when all of God's promises will be complete in Christ. And because so many prophecies have already been fulfilled in Christ, we have hope that God will fulfill His every promise through Christ.

As we wait in the tension between the cross and glory, we do not wait without hope. This Advent season points us to Christ's first coming, but it also points us to the Second Advent, when Christ will come again. Because we know that Christ has already come, we can know with confidence that Christ will return. But just like the disappointment we may feel after Christmas Day, we might wrestle with feelings of discouragement and discontentment while waiting for Christ's return. Yet we can rekindle our hope by looking back at what God has done through Christ and what He will do when Jesus returns. We can rejoice in what has been fulfilled while anticipating and hoping in what has not yet been fulfilled.

Our hearts find hope and joy by coming to God's Word, God's special revelation to us. Because of Christ's grace and the gift of the Holy Spirit, God speaks to us through His Word, and we respond with obedience, delight, and praise. So, in this Advent season, rest in God's promises through His Word and look ahead to when Jesus will completely fulfill each and every one.

## QUESTIONS

**1** Read Luke 24:44. How is God's Word all about Jesus?

QUESTIONS CONTINUE ▶

**2** How does the truth that God has fulfilled many prophecies in Christ foster your hope?

**3** How can you look ahead this Advent season? How does God's Word benefit you as you look ahead?

## Notes

# Week 1, Day 7
# APPLICATION

*Before we begin a new week of study, take some time to apply and share the truths of Scripture you learned this week. Here are a few ideas of how you could do this:*

- Schedule a meet-up with a friend to share what you are learning from God's Word.

- Use these prompts to journal or pray through what God is revealing to you through your study of His Word.

*Lord, I feel…*

*Lord, You are…*

*Lord, forgive me for…*

*Lord, help me with…*

- Spend time worshiping God in a way that is meaningful to you, whether that is taking a walk in nature, painting, drawing, singing, etc.

- Paraphrase the Scripture you read this week.

- Use a study Bible or commentary to help you answer questions that came up as you read this week's Scripture.

- Use highlighters to mark the places you see the metanarrative of Scripture in one or more of the passages of Scripture that you read this week. (See The Metanarrative of Scripture on page 174.)

# PROPHECIES
## FULFILLED BY JESUS OR INVOLVING JESUS
*in The Book of Matthew*

| PASSAGE | EVENT | FULFILLMENT OF |
|---------|-------|----------------|
| MATTHEW 1:20 – 23 | Jesus is born of a virgin and named Immanuel. | ISAIAH 7:14 |
| MATTHEW 2:5 – 6 | Jesus is born in Bethlehem, in the land of Judea. | MICAH 5:2 |
| MATTHEW 2:14 – 15 | Jesus's parents take Him to Egypt to hide from Herod. | HOSEA 11:1 |
| MATTHEW 2:16 – 18 | Herod kills all the boys two years old and younger to keep the promised Messiah from living. | JEREMIAH 31:15 |
| MATTHEW 3:1 – 3 | John the Baptist prepares the way for Jesus. | ISAIAH 40:3 |
| MATTHEW 4:12 – 17 | Jesus goes to Zebulun and Naphtali before starting His ministry. | ISAIAH 9:1 – 2 |

| PASSAGE | EVENT | FULFILLMENT OF |
|---|---|---|
| MATTHEW 8:16 – 17 | *Jesus heals the sick and demon-possessed.* | ISAIAH 53:4 |
| MATTHEW 10:34 – 36 | *Jesus's message and the new way of life He calls people to bring conflict.* | MICAH 7:6 |
| MATTHEW 12:14 – 21 | *Jesus's ministry is marked by humility.* | ISAIAH 42:1 – 4 |
| MATTHEW 13:13 – 15 | *The people do not listen or understand Jesus's parables.* | ISAIAH 6:9 – 10 |
| MATTHEW 21:1 – 5 | *Jesus rides on a donkey into Jerusalem.* | ZECHARIAH 9:9 |
| MATTHEW 26 – 27 | *Jesus is beaten, mocked, and killed without retaliating.* | ISAIAH 52:13 – 53:12 |
| MATTHEW 26:31 | *Jesus predicts His disciples will fall away from Him.* | ZECHARIAH 13:7 |
| MATTHEW 27:3 – 10 | *The thirty pieces of silver that Judas received for betraying Jesus are used to purchase a field.* | ZECHARIAH 11:12 – 13 |

*Week 2*

# Priest

JESUS IS OUR GREAT HIGH PRIEST

WHO GIVES US PEACE.

*Candle Lighting*

# Peace

2 · 1

Today, we light the peace candle, remembering
that Jesus, our Great High Priest, secured peace for
us — not just in our daily lives but for forever.

FATHER,

As we light the peace candle today, we thank You that You gave
us Jesus to be our peace. We praise You for sending Your Son to
take on our sin and shame and pay the price we never could so
that we could be with You forever. Because of Jesus, nothing in
this world can ultimately harm us, for we have salvation in You.

WE PRAY THIS IN YOUR SON'S PRECIOUS NAME,

AMEN

# Memory
# Verse

2 · 1

Though your sins are scarlet,
they will be as white as snow;
though they are crimson red,
they will be like wool.

ISAIAH 1:18B

Christ, our Priest, brings us before the Father as holy vessels.

68

# What Is the Role of a Priest?

**READ LEVITICUS 8 – 10, NUMBERS 3:1 – 10**

Every year, as the holiday season approaches, our to-do lists grow, and the preparations for Christmas seem to multiply. From meals to gifts to travel, we spend precious time and effort preparing for Christmas Day. But in this season of Advent, do we spend as much time preparing our hearts for the celebration of our Savior's birth? This theme of preparation will mark our time in the Word this week as we look at the role of the priests in the Old Testament and how this role points to our perfect and better Priest, Jesus.

In order to fully appreciate Christ's role as Priest in our lives, we must understand the origins and purpose of this role. This might not seem particularly festive, but this is one of the roles Jesus embodies, and it should be celebrated just like we celebrate His roles as King and Messiah. Understanding the Old Testament role of the priest enables us to see the beautiful preparations God initiated to pave the way for Jesus to fulfill the role completely and perfectly.

The role of the priest was initiated after the Israelites left their bondage in Egypt and the Lord led them to Mount Sinai in the wilderness. It was there that they made their camp while Moses climbed the mountain to receive the Law. On the mountain, he also received the specifications for the building of the tabernacle, the anointing of the priests, and the sacrificial system (Exodus 25–31). In Exodus 25:8–9a, the Lord says to Moses, "They are to make a sanctuary for me so that I may dwell among them. You must make it according to all that I show you." The beauty of the tabernacle and the priestly garments were meant to reflect the glory of the Lord and evoke worship from the people. The consecration and cleansing of the priests to their sacred position displayed God's holiness and mankind's inability for perfection in their sinful state.

The office of the priesthood in the Old Testament held great honor, but more importantly, it held great responsibility. Priests filled a God-ordained position that enabled the people to seek forgiveness of sin and thus withhold the wrath of God from year to year. Leviticus 8–10 details the consecration of the priests. Moses himself would not be a priest, but he was God's chosen leader to anoint the tabernacle and the priests who served there. Numbers 3 also details how the tribe of Levi was chosen to assist Aaron in caring for the tabernacle and its furnishings. This was important because God's presence dwelt in the tabernacle, and it was the center of the Israelite camp and nation.

Leviticus 8 recounts the consecration of Aaron and his sons. These men were chosen by God. They were not chosen due to merit but because God had a plan to use them and their future generations for His glory. As these men came forward, they were first washed and then anointed with oil by Moses, which is a similar picture of the anointing of the Holy Spirit. This anointing marked them as set apart for God's purpose. A sin offering was required to atone for the sin of the priests, and a burnt offering was given as a pleasing aroma to the Lord. Then they were instructed to remain within the tent for seven days until their ordination was complete.

On the eighth day, the priests began the ministry of the tabernacle. The high priest was given the charge of atoning for the sin of the entire nation. Before he could fulfill that role, he had to first cleanse himself and offer a sacrifice for his own sin. Once complete, he offered the sin, burnt, grain, and fellowship offerings on behalf of the people (Leviticus 1–7). Aaron blessed the nation, and God accepted the offering of the people as His glory consumed the sacrifice in fire. This led the people to great worship. This same process would be followed for hundreds of years until the arrival of Christ, the final Priest, made it obsolete (Hebrews 8:13).

The contrast of the beautiful priestly garments with the spattered blood of the sacrificed animals should cause us to pause and consider what the Lord wanted the Israelites, and us, to learn from this process. Hebrews 9:22 says, "without the shedding of blood there is no forgiveness." God ordained the sacrifice of innocent animals to atone for sin and delay His wrath. He ordained sinful men to enter the Holy of Holies, the place where His presence dwelt in the tabernacle, to remind mankind of their dependence on yearly atonement. Sin requires payment, and God provided a temporary process until His permanent solution, Jesus, arrived.

---

*Our Great High Priest, Jesus, has made us members of this royal priesthood. We now proclaim Him with our lives.*

In Leviticus 10, we read how God gave a charge to the high priests to be holy and teach His statutes to the nation. Holiness and obedience were imperative. Aaron's sons Nadab and Abihu learned this lesson the hard way when they took the commands of the Lord and the sacred tabernacle lightly. Aaron and his remaining sons were charged to live lives of holiness, set apart for the ministry of the Lord. They were to model this for the nation and lead them to desire holiness and lives that reflected their love for and devotion to the God who saved them.

As believers, we are also called to holiness. We should look different from the world. Sin is deadly and causes separation from our holy God. But Christ, our Priest, brings us before the Father as holy vessels through the sacrifice of His life. During this Christmas season, may we seek holiness amidst the commercial focus of the holiday. First Peter 2:9 tells us, "But you are a chosen race, a royal priesthood, a holy nation, a people for his possession, so that you may proclaim the praises of the one who called you out of darkness into his marvelous light." Our Great High Priest, Jesus, has made us members of this royal priesthood. We now proclaim Him with our lives.

# QUESTIONS

**1** Why was the priesthood important to the nation of Israel, and how did it display mankind's need for a Savior?

QUESTIONS CONTINUE ▶

**2**  Why did the priests have to atone for their sin before atoning for the sin of the nation? How did God show His acceptance of the sacrifice? Why is this important?

**3**  What are some practical ways you can proclaim Christ during this Advent season? As a "royal priest" in God's kingdom (1 Peter 2:9), how should your life be marked by holiness?

**Notes**

Jesus was the final, once-for-all-time sacrifice.

WEEK 2 / DAY 3

# Our Need for a Priest

**READ LEVITICUS 16, HEBREWS 7:23–28**

As you plan for Christmas, what usually takes the most preparation? It may be getting a tree, unboxing your cherished nativity set, or preparing that ever-important Christmas meal. Whatever it might be, we all take great pains in our preparations because Christmas is important, special, and worthy of our time and effort. This sentiment was the same for the Israelites as they observed the Day of Atonement. No day was more important or holy in their calendar year. And no role was more important than that of the high priest. Without him, atonement could not be made. Israel needed a priest, and as we study today, we will see how desperately we need one, as well.

Yesterday, we began the second week of Advent by studying the role of the priest. The role of the high priest was given to Aaron and his two younger sons, Eleazar and Ithamar, after the death of his two older sons, Nadab and Abihu (Leviticus 10). The role was generational. A high priest held the office for his lifetime, and when he died, the role passed to his son. Leviticus 16:32 says, "The priest who is anointed and ordained to serve as high priest in place of his father will make atonement." We also read in Hebrews 7:23, "Now many have become Levitical priests, since they are prevented by death from remaining in office." These verses remind us that these men were finite. Though they held an immensely important role, they, too, would die. But God used these men for the good of His people and His plan of redemption. Sin had to be paid for then, and it must be paid for now.

------------------ ✦ ------------------

## *That precious baby, born on Christmas Day so long ago, now gives us life.*

------------------

Preparations for the Day of Atonement were crucial and extensive. As we read the Leviticus 16 account, there are likely many unfamiliar terms. Defining these terms helps us unwrap this day and understand its significance in the life of Israel and how Jesus came to fulfill each and every aspect. Each year, the Day of Atonement occurred on the tenth day of the seventh month. Just as we know that Christmas falls on December 25 each year, this most holy day never came as a shock to the Israelites. It was on this day that the nation sought forgiveness for their sin. With each passing year, the wrath of God required atonement to stay His wrath until the next year.

On the Day of Atonement, the high priest had to first cleanse himself, then clothe himself in the priestly garments. Once enrobed, he would offer a sin offering and a burnt offering. The priestly garments represented the function of the high priest as the mediator between God and man. They were a reflection of the glory and beauty due to God. Once the high priest was cleansed and his sin atoned, he could then offer on behalf of the people. The sacrifice for

the nation included both live and sacrificed animals with very specific instructions.

To atone for the nation's sin, two goats were brought before the high priest, and a lot was cast to see which would be the sacrifice and which would be the scapegoat. The term "scapegoat" likely sounds familiar as it is used even today to describe someone who bears the blame for others. This goat literally bore the sin of the nation as Aaron confessed over it "all the Israelites' iniquities and rebellious acts—all their sins" (Leviticus 16:21). The goat was then led into the wilderness and released there as a picture of removing the sin and guilt of the nation from the presence of the Lord and the camp.

The second goat was sacrificed, and its blood was placed on the mercy seat. This was the golden lid that covered the ark of the covenant where the Ten Commandments were kept. God said in Exodus 25:22, "I will meet with you there above the mercy seat." Behind the curtain in the inner tent, above the mercy seat, the God of the universe dwelt with His people. It was there that He accepted their sacrifice and forgave them for another year. This day was to be a permanent statute for the nation as their sin must be atoned for annually. God ordained this sacrificial system in His great mercy, yet all these preparations and rituals were not enough to completely wipe away the debt of Israel's sin, nor ours.

Thankfully, God did make a way for our sin debt to be wiped away through His Son, Jesus. When Jesus was born on that blessed Christmas night, the stars shone brightly, the shepherds worshiped joyfully, and Mary treasured each moment in her heart (Luke 2:19–20). But that beautiful baby had the greatest purpose and mission in history. He grew into a man who would fulfill the role of High Priest perfectly. He had no need to cleanse Himself because He was sinless. God had come to the earth to physically walk among His people. Jesus became the mercy seat when He took on flesh and dwelt among us (John 1:14). Jesus was the scapegoat who bore our sin and shame on the cross. And Jesus was the final, once-for-all-time sacrifice as His blood flowed from calvary and covered us in forgiveness (Hebrews 10:10).

As our High Priest, Jesus took Himself behind the curtain in the most holy place. There, He offered His own blood as permanent atonement for our sin. God established the Day of Atonement as a permanent statute for the nation of Israel. Jesus replaced that statute with Himself and delivered the crushing blow to sin once and for all. That precious baby, born on Christmas Day so long ago, now gives us life—abundant life here on earth and a glorious eternity in His presence (John 10:10, Revelation 21:3). This Christmas, may our hearts celebrate the triumphant work of our Priest, Jesus, who gave His life to return us to the presence of the Father.

## QUESTIONS

**1** What does the Day of Atonement teach you about God's character and the seriousness of sin? Why do we need atonement for our sin?

QUESTIONS CONTINUE ▶

**2** Read the verses below, and explain how Jesus fulfilled each aspect of the Day of Atonement. Why is this important?

PRIEST (HEBREWS 7:24, 26 – 27)

SCAPEGOAT (2 CORINTHIANS 5:21)

SACRIFICE (HEBREWS 10:12 – 15)

MERCY SEAT (ROMANS 3:23 – 26)

**3** Is Jesus the "permanent statute" of your life (Leviticus 16:29–34)? If so, take some time to reflect on the moment of your salvation and your walk with the Lord since then, and record a prayer of thanksgiving and worship to our sacrificial Priest. If not, take some time to reflect on what you learned today, and write down any questions you still have.

## Notes

Jesus is our Priest and King, and he sits on the throne of our hearts.

# The Anticipated Priest

**READ PSALM 110, I SAMUEL 2:22–35**

Christmas is a time of great anticipation. Children look forward to the magical season with the presents they hope to receive and the treats they hope to eat. Adults look forward to time spent with family members they might only see once a year. And the world, though gripped by sin, exhales in the hope of a season of rest and goodwill toward others. Anticipation marked that very first Christmas, as well, but for a very different reason. For thousands of years, the children of Israel awaited their Messiah. They awaited a Priest who could atone for their sin permanently and perfectly. On that starry night in Bethlehem, the world exhaled because the Priest had arrived.

As we have studied previously, the sacrificial system, the tabernacle, and the priests were all created to reflect the glory of God, atone for sin, evoke worship from the people, and display their obedience. But most importantly, it provided a way for God to dwell with man, though veiled by a curtain. This sacred process was always meant to be a temporary means to an end. It was always meant to make hearts anticipate the perfection to come. Though temporary, the priests were called to be holy men who led Israel to be holy. But they failed miserably.

Various places across the Old Testament detail the inability of priests to fulfill their roles. We have already read about the death of Aaron's sons, Nadab and Abihu, who disrespected the tabernacle (Leviticus 10:2). Today, we read about the two sons of Eli, who was the high priest in 1 Samuel 2. His sons, Hophni and Phinehas, openly sinned against the Lord and misused the offerings provided for the priests. The Lord required their life. But even in this hard story, God provided a glimpse of the anticipated, obedient, and perfect Priest in 1 Samuel 2:35: "Then I will raise up a faithful priest for myself. He will do whatever is in my heart and mind. I will establish a lasting dynasty for him, and he will walk before my anointed one for all time."

Other places in Scripture call out the priests for their failure to impart knowledge and holiness to the people. Because the priests forgot the Law, God promised to forget them and reject them as servants (Hosea 4:6). When they chose not to listen or honor the Lord's name, He cursed and rebuked them, rejected their descendants, and had them removed just like the waste from the animal sacrifices (Malachi 2:1–3). Priest after priest, failure upon failure. None were good enough; none were holy enough. The world longed for and anticipated a priest who was "holy, innocent, undefiled, separated from sinners, and exalted above the heavens" (Hebrews 7:26).

One of the greatest anticipatory passages of our coming Priest is Psalm 110. This is known as a royal psalm. Written by Israel's King David, this psalm does not simply describe David's accomplishments as king; it describes the eternal King who would sit on the Davidic throne forever (2 Samuel 7:16). The nation of Israel sang this psalm to celebrate God's covenant with David. But there are several striking distinctions in this psalm that set Jesus apart as a superior

Priest, one who would complete the mission of His Father perfectly.

◆

## Christmas is a time when we can celebrate that Christ took on flesh and came to conquer sin and death.

The first distinction is found in Psalm 110:1, which says, "This is the declaration of the Lord to my Lord: 'Sit at my right hand until I make your enemies your footstool.'" God is declaring Jesus's deity when He calls Jesus "Lord." Because of His deity, Jesus fulfills the Davidic covenant as the One who would sit on the throne forever and defeat His enemies, thus making them a footstool. Secondly, Psalm 110:4 tells us, "The Lord has sworn an oath and will not take it back: 'You are a priest forever according to the pattern of Melchizedek.'" Not only is Jesus the eternal King, but He is also the eternal Priest. These dual roles have significant implications we will discuss further tomorrow, along with the significance of the name Melchizedek, but here in this royal psalm, we see that our anticipated Priest will also wear a crown and declare a new covenant to include Jews and Gentiles.

The prophet and priest Zechariah, who prophesied to the group of Israelites that returned from exile, also spoke about this idea of a priest on the throne. Zechariah 6:13 says, "Yes, he will build the Lord's temple; he will bear royal splendor and will sit on his throne and rule. There will be a priest on his throne, and there will be peaceful counsel between the two of them." Jesus would come and perfect the priesthood, making the final sacrifice required for sin. He would then sit on the throne and rule over the temple built on the foundation of His sacrifice. That temple is not one made of brick and mortar but one made of believers who declare Christ as their Savior (1 Peter 2:5). We are now the temple where the Lord dwells. Jesus is our Priest and King, and He sits on the throne of our hearts.

Anticipation looks a little different for believers today. Christ has already come, but now we await His promised return. Christmas is a time when we can celebrate that Christ took on flesh and came to conquer sin and death. It is also a celebration and anticipation for His return when He will make all things new (Revelation 21:5). As we wait for that day, the Lord has given us all we need to love and serve Him well. We are His temple, and He has given us a mission to share the good news of the gospel. Philippians 3:20 reminds us why our anticipation is great; it is because "our citizenship is in heaven, and we eagerly wait for a Savior from there, the Lord Jesus Christ." May Christmas be a time when we joyfully prepare for Christ's return and anticipate the day we dwell with Him forever.

# QUESTIONS

**1** How did the sacrificial system prompt anticipation for a better Priest? Why did the human priests fail so badly, and why was Jesus victorious?

QUESTIONS CONTINUE ▸

**2** Why is Jesus's role as Priest unique in comparison to the earthly priests? How do the prophecies of His priesthood display God's sovereignty?

**3** Read the verses below. As we wait and anticipate Christ's second coming, how are believers called to live?

ROMANS 12:1–2

TITUS 2:11–13

# Notes

Jesus is both the High Priest and the sacrifice.

# Jesus: The Great High Priest

**READ GENESIS 14:17–20, HEBREWS 1:3, HEBREWS 6:19–7:7, HEBREWS 9:24–28**

Every Christmas, there is that one family member who enjoys having fun with their gift-giving. Maybe they create an elaborate scavenger hunt to locate your gift, maybe they hand you the present exasperatingly wrapped inside another present, or possibly they give you a key to unlock a gift. Whichever method is used, the anticipation of the gift is heightened due to the events and obstacles surrounding it. As that first Christmas approached in Bethlehem, God had given clue after clue to His people that the Messiah was coming. With each passing year, the hope of the Savior grew. When He finally arrived, He was not what the world expected, but He was exactly what we needed. He was, and is, our Great High Priest.

The role of the high priest had great implications for the Jews. But for those of us who are not Jewish by birth, the necessity of a high priest can be difficult to understand. However, just like that family member who likes to give clues or a key to your gift, God has given both Jews and Gentiles all we need to understand this important role of Christ. One of those keys is the book of Hebrews. It is like no other in the New Testament as it specifically unlocks the mysteries of the priesthood and declares Jesus as the Great High Priest for all mankind. Specifically, it will help us understand our need for a High Priest and Jesus's superiority.

Yesterday, we read Psalm 110 and were introduced to a man named Melchizedek, as well as Jesus's dual roles of King and Priest. This ancient man and these dual roles tell us much about our Messiah and His fulfillment of the priesthood. Melchizedek is mentioned in only three places in Scripture — Genesis 14, Psalm 110, and the book of Hebrews. Genesis 14:18 tells us that Melchizedek was "king of Salem…he was a priest to God Most High." Salem was the ancient name for Jerusalem, and Melchizedek held the role of king and priest of God Most High in this important town. He was held in great honor and esteem, as evidenced by the offering Abram gave him. He was no ordinary man but instead singled out as a forerunner of Christ.

Hebrews further explains who Melchizedek was by explaining that he was a king of peace and a king of righteousness with no beginning or end (Hebrews 7:2–3). He resembled the Son of God. Psalm 110:4 affirms this by stating Christ is a priest forever in the order of Melchizedek. Some believe Melchizedek was a preincarnate appearance of Christ, while others believe he was a "type" of Christ, which can be defined as a person, object, or institution that serves as a shadow and points forward to the true substance of Christ. While that aspect of Melchizedek's identity will remain a mystery, we do know that Melchizedek pointed to Jesus and gave the Jews a glimpse of what to expect in the Messiah. The Savior of the world would be both a king and a priest.

The idea that one man held both the kingship and the priesthood would puzzle a devout Jew. The roles of priest and king were separate and distinct in the Jewish nation. The priests came from the tribe of Levi, while the kings came from the tribe of Judah. No king entered the temple to make atonement for the nation, and no priest sat on the throne to rule. Scripture clearly tells us that Jesus descended from the line of Judah and fulfilled the covenant made to David that his "throne will be established forever" (2 Samuel 7:16, Revelation 5:5). As a physical member of the tribe of Judah, Jesus could not be from the tribe of Levi. Instead, He was a priest of God Most High in the order of Melchizedek. God alone ordained Jesus's priesthood. And through these roles, He accomplished what no king or priest before or after Him could finish.

On that first Christmas night, this small child resting in a manger came to fulfill the role of Great High Priest. While the Jews hoped for a conquering king to destroy the Romans, Jesus came to conquer sin and death. Year after year, the Levitical priests sacrificed animals to seek atonement for sin, but Jesus, our Great High Priest, destroyed sin completely. He did this by taking Himself behind the curtain and offering His own spotless blood as a one-time sacrifice for all (Hebrews 9:26). Jesus is both the High Priest and the sacrifice. Jesus made atonement for our sins, and we now enjoy God's presence as we await His return.

Jesus's roles as High Priest and King are intricately connected. One does not exist without the other. We will discuss Jesus as King in more detail next week, but for now, it is important to understand that only the Son of God could hold these two roles perfectly and complete them absolutely. The author of Hebrews encapsulates these roles in Hebrews 1:3b, which says, "After making purification for sins, he sat down at the right hand of the Majesty on high." As our Priest, Jesus made purification for sin. As our King, He sat down at the right hand of God. To sit down in first-century culture signaled that the work was complete. Jesus completed His work when He fulfilled His role as High Priest, atoned for all sin on the cross, and rose victoriously.

When Jesus came to dwell among mankind, He gave us the gift of eternal life through His completed work. But He also gave us the gift of knowing Him and unwrapping His character throughout our lives. With each new day, we can know our Savior more intimately and proclaim Him to others. The process of becoming more like Jesus is called sanctification. This journey is a gift that Jesus gives us to make us look less like the world and more like Him. This Christmas, the gift we can give our Savior is to be holy as He is holy. We turn our eyes toward Him and hope for the day when He takes us to the new heaven and new earth. There, sin will be no more, and the temple will be the "Lord God the Almighty and the Lamb" (Revelation 21:22).

# QUESTIONS

**1** Who was Melchizedek? Why is understanding his role important in understanding Jesus's role as High Priest?

QUESTIONS CONTINUE ▶

**2** Why are Christ's roles as both Priest and King significant? How did Jesus accomplish what the Levitical priests could not?

**3** How can you grow in sanctification? What action steps can you take this Advent season to look more like Jesus to a watching world?

## Notes

The good news of the gospel is that Jesus came to save the world.

# Jesus: Our Priest

## READ HEBREWS 10:11–14, HEBREWS 10:19–23, EPHESIANS 2:11–22

Christmas is a time filled with love, anticipation, hope, and joy. But even in this happiest of seasons, feelings of envy creep in. Longing and coveting can overtake our hearts as we desire the gift someone else received. We may find ourselves wanting the same joy the gift brought to them. For those of us not born of Jewish heritage, the same could be said of the Jewish Messiah who was born that first Christmas night. To outsiders, it could easily seem like perhaps this Savior came to fulfill something for God's chosen people, and everyone else was simply excluded. Though they may not have realized it, the hearts of mankind envied this nation that now had the perfect Priest to atone for sin, as they longed for a Priest of their own.

The good news of the gospel is that Jesus came to save the world. Greeks, or Gentiles, do not have to be jealous of the Jews' Messiah because He came to be their Savior, as well. Romans 10:12 tells us, "there is no distinction between Jew and Greek, because the same Lord of all richly blesses all who call on him." Before Christ came, Greeks were excluded from the promises of God and without hope (Ephesians 2:12). However, Ephesians 2:13–14b tells us, "But now in Christ Jesus, you who were far away have been brought near by the blood of Christ. For he is our peace, who made both groups one and tore down the dividing wall of hostility." There is no need for envy because He is our Savior, too. He brought peace by becoming both High Priest and sacrifice, making atonement for all.

---

## We boldly walk into God's presence, robed in the righteousness of Christ, to worship and petition our heavenly Father.

---

Over the past four days, we have briefly studied the Levitical priesthood and seen how Jesus came to fulfill the role of High Priest uniquely and perfectly. This role has great implications for both Jews and Greeks as Jesus offered Himself as the spotless sacrifice once and for all. While the Levitical priests entered the temple day after day, Jesus entered one time, offered Himself once, and sanctified those who believe forever (Hebrews 10:11–14). Clothed in the robes of righteousness, Jesus, our Priest, willingly went behind the curtain into the Holy of Holies and gave His life. On the cross, His body bore the pain, agony, and wrath of God that mankind deserved for their sin. It is through His torn and bleeding body that we draw near to the Father. The curtain in the temple has been torn in two by our Great High Priest, and we now have access to the presence of God Almighty.

For believers, access to the Father comes through the salvation Christ provides and the indwelling of the Holy Spirit. Jesus destroyed our need for the priesthood and the sacrificial system with His death and resurrection. The Apostle Paul tells us in Galatians 3:13a, "Christ redeemed us from the curse of the law by becoming a curse for us." Jesus tore down the barrier between God and man, and "in him we have boldness and confident access through faith in him" (Ephesians 3:12). We boldly walk into God's presence, robed in the righteousness of Christ, to worship and petition our heavenly Father.

Believers draw near to the presence of the Father in a way the ancient Hebrews could not. Their hope for forgiveness rested in equally sinful men and their ability to follow the sacrificial instructions. But Jesus, our Great High Priest, has sprinkled our hearts clean with His blood of atonement. His completed work heals us inwardly and makes us right before the Father eternally. Envy has no place in our hearts because the God of Abraham, Isaac, and Jacob is our God, too. The promises and covenants He made thousands of years ago find their completion in Christ. Through His sacrifice, we are heirs of the promise. Galatians 3:29 proclaims, "And if you belong to Christ, then you are Abraham's seed, heirs according to the promise." The nation God promised to Abraham so long ago includes all who call on the name of Jesus for salvation. Christian Jews and Greeks alike will worship Jesus around the throne one day.

Our Great High Priest enables us to hold fast and stand firm in our confession of hope until He comes again for His children. Our confession is that Jesus Christ is Lord. We hope in

His salvation, forgiveness, and return. He is the Priest of our hearts, interceding on our behalf before the Father in heaven (Hebrews 7:25). One day, He will return for us and take us home to the new heaven and new earth. The Apostle John saw this glorious day in Revelation 7:9–10 when he said:

> After this I looked, and there was a vast multitude from every nation, tribe, people, and language, which no one could number, standing before the throne and before the Lamb. They were clothed in white robes with palm branches in their hands. And they cried out in a loud voice: Salvation belongs to our God, who is seated on the throne, and to the Lamb!

Salvation is for all who call on the name of Jesus Christ. Believers are now members of God's holy nation and chosen people (1 Peter 2:9). The gift of the Savior that first Christmas night was not just for the Jews but for the world. This Advent season, we celebrate that Jesus is our Priest, and we worship the sacrificial Lamb who sits on the throne.

# QUESTIONS

**1** How does Jesus provide access to the Father? How did He destroy the Levitical priesthood and sacrificial system?

QUESTIONS CONTINUE ▶

**2**  What is your confession of faith? In what ways do you hold fast and stand firm in your salvation?

**3**  Write out each of the verses listed below. How do they remind you that Jesus is your Priest and that you belong to the family of God?

GALATIANS 3:26

EPHESIANS 2:19–20

PHILIPPIANS 3:20

## Notes

*Before we begin a new week of study, take some time to apply and share the truths of Scripture you learned this week. Here are a few ideas of how you could do this:*

- Schedule a meet-up with a friend to share what you are learning from God's Word.

- Use these prompts to journal or pray through what God is revealing to you through your study of His Word.

*Lord, I feel…*

_____

_____

_____

*Lord, You are…*

_____

_____

_____

*Lord, forgive me for…*

_____

_____

_____

*Lord, help me with…*

- Spend time worshiping God in a way that is meaningful to you, whether that is taking a walk in nature, painting, drawing, singing, etc.

- Paraphrase the Scripture you read this week.

- Use a study Bible or commentary to help you answer questions that came up as you read this week's Scripture.

- Use highlighters to mark the places you see the metanarrative of Scripture in one or more of the passages of Scripture that you read this week. (See The Metanarrative of Scripture on page 174.)

# JESUS'S FULFILLMENT OF THE
# PRIESTHOOD

**Turban:** The white turban covering the head of the priest signified submission to the Lord. It also held the diadem with a band of blue lace to bear the iniquity of the people before God (Exodus 28:36–38).

**Plate (Diadem):** Made of gold and placed on the front of the turban, the plate was engraved with the words "Holy to the Lord." It removed from God's presence any wrongdoing and made Israel's worship acceptable to the Lord (Exodus 39:30–31).

**Tunic:** The tunic was white to represent the cleansing of the priest. It was made of fine woven linen and worn under the robe as an undergarment (Exodus 28:39–43).

**Breastpiece:** The breastpiece sat on top of the ephod. It displayed twelve precious stones, which represented each tribe of Israel. As the high priest sacrificed, the stones symbolized the presence of the nation before God to atone for their sin (Exodus 28:15–30).

**Ephod:** Similar to a vest, the ephod was worn over the robe. It was ornate and inscribed with the names of the twelve tribes of Israel, with six names on one shoulder piece and six names on the other. Both shoulder pieces were made of onyx and used to fasten the ephod (Exodus 28:6–14).

**Robe:** The robe was worn over the tunic and had small bells sewn on the bottom. The bells served a couple of purposes: 1) The sound reminded the people of the sacred work the priest did on their behalf. 2) The sound "alerted" God that the priest was coming to sacrifice before Him so that he would not die in the presence of the Holy God (Exodus 28:31–35).

**Crown of Thorns**: This crown was meant to mock Jesus. Though it was not gold and did not read "Holy to the Lord" like the diadem of the high priest, it was a symbol of humility as Jesus became obedient to death. His crown did not need to declare His holiness, for His life had already done it (Matthew 27:29, Mark 15:17, John 19:2, Philippians 2:7–8).

**Sign on the Cross:** The sign that hung on the cross above Jesus's head read "King of the Jews." Like the crown of thorns, though it was meant to mock Jesus, it became a symbol of Jesus's submission to the Father as He willingly went to His death on our behalf. Jesus was and is our Priest and King, not just for the Jews but for all who call on His name (Matthew 27:37, Luke 23:38, John 19:19).

**Pierced Side and Nail Wounds:** Each year, the priest entered the presence of the Lord with the names of the twelve tribes on the breastpiece and the ephod to represent the repentance of the nation before the Lord. Jesus entered the presence of the Father with a pierced side and the wounds from nails in His hands and feet to declare complete payment of sin for mankind. Jesus stands before the Father on our behalf with wounds that bring us eternal atonement (John 19:34–37, Isaiah 53:5, 1 Peter 2:24).

**Robe:** As the guards stripped Jesus and cloaked Him in a robe of purple to humiliate and taunt Him, they could not see the robe of righteousness He already wore in His perfect nature. Jesus conquered sin and death, and the angels in heaven rejoiced as the King returned and took His rightful, royal place next to the Father (Matthew 27:28, Mark 15:17–20, John 19:2, Philippians 2:9–11, Isaiah 53:12).

**Crushed Body:** When Jesus was crucified on the cross, He wore no white linen tunic to signify purification. He was the pure and spotless lamb of God. As He bore our sin, naked on the tree, He took Himself behind the curtain of the Holy of Holies and gave His life to save sinners (Isaiah 53:11b, Hebrews 7:24–25).

---

*Hebrews 10:19–23*

*Therefore, brothers and sisters, since we have boldness to enter the sanctuary through the blood of Jesus—he has inaugurated for us a new and living way through the curtain (that is, through his flesh)—and since we have a great high priest over the house of God, let us draw near with a true heart in full assurance of faith, with our hearts sprinkled clean from an evil conscience and our bodies washed in pure water. Let us hold on to the confession of our hope without wavering, since he who promised is faithful.*

Week 3

# King

JESUS IS THE KING OF KINGS

WHO FILLS US WITH JOY.

*Candle Lighting*

# Joy

3 · 1

Today, we light the joy candle, remembering that Jesus, our King, invites us into His kingdom, which is filled with joy.

FATHER,

This world is filled with so much sorrow and sadness. However, we praise You that You are a God of joy! When we are sad, we can remember the joy of our salvation. We can remember that You care for and love us so much that You sent Your one and only Son to pay the price for our sins so that we could live with You forever. Thank You for giving us the joy of the world and the hope that brings us on our saddest days.

WE PRAY THIS IN YOUR SON'S PRECIOUS NAME,

AMEN

# Memory Verse

3 : 1

Enter his gates with thanksgiving and his courts with praise. Give thanks to him and bless his name.

PSALM 100:4

Jesus is the perfect
embodiment of kingship.

# What Is the Role of a King?

READ DEUTERONOMY 17:14–20

There is something fascinating about royalty. We are drawn to the glamorous clothes, complex drama, and power-hungry decisions that plague dynasties throughout history. Many people enjoy watching shows and reading books with kings and queens as the main characters. We might feel so enraptured by nobility because it feels so distant from our lives today. Few monarchies still exist, and of those that do, most are little more than figureheads rather than the kings of the past who often possessed absolute power. Yet, since before the world began, there has been a King who rules over all of creation, and His power continues to shape our lives today and into eternity.

This all-powerful King, God, made Himself known to a man named Abram and established a covenant and a relationship with him. In Genesis 17:5–6, God said to Abram, "Your name will no longer be Abram; your name will be Abraham, for I will make you the father of many nations. I will make you extremely fruitful and will make nations and kings come from you." And God remained faithful to His promises, making Abraham the father of a great nation that later came to be known as Israel.

Several centuries later, however, the Israelites found themselves under the rule of an oppressive Pharaoh in a foreign country rather than under the kingship of a descendant of

Abraham. But still, God remembered His people, sending Moses to save them from the evil kingship of Pharaoh. Once they were delivered, the Israelites began making their way to the Promised Land, where God would establish them as a nation, just as He promised Abraham. And though God was sufficient to be their King, He knew His people would reject His kingship, desiring instead an earthly king like the nations surrounding them (1 Samuel 8:6–8). So, in His infinite wisdom, God provided the Israelites with specific instructions for the characteristics of a future king in Deuteronomy 17:14–20.

Why did Israel need a king at all? They already had the true King of heaven and earth on their side—the One who led them out of Egypt, parted the Red Sea, and sent manna from heaven as they wandered in the wilderness. But even though God provided for them as a good King, the people were quick to forget. Soon after God parted the Red Sea, the people complained about His lack of provision and wished to go back to the slavery of Egypt. When God sent manna, the people greedily stockpiled extra instead of trusting God to bring them what they needed each day. Even before the Israelites requested an earthly king, their hearts were far from God, their true King. God had promised nations and kings to come through Abraham's descendants, but Israel wanted more. They wanted a king who could fight their battles. They wanted to be like "all the other nations" (1 Samuel 8:20). In their sin, they rejected God's good kingship for their own desires long before they ever asked for an earthly king.

So, in Deuteronomy 17:14–20, God lists three specific requirements for the future king of Israel. First, he must be chosen by God (Deuteronomy 17:15a). After all, it was God who truly knew what Israel needed, and out of His great love, God desired to provide for His people.

Allowing God to choose Israel's leader would be an act of obedience and trust. Second, the king must come from the family line of Israel (Deuteronomy 17:15b). Though Israel was surrounded by foreign nations, it was always meant to be a nation that was set apart to worship God alone. Thus, any future king of Israel must be from the tribes of Israel and not a foreigner. Third, the king must obey and trust in God alone (Deuteronomy 17:16–20). He was not to acquire many horses, many wives, or much wealth for Himself. Instead, He was to trust and remain devoted to God alone.

These are not the requirements we would expect from a king. Most would imagine a king would need to be a great military leader, wise, strong, handsome, and brave. God, however, does not require any of those characteristics in a king—only faithfulness to Him.

---

*We live under the kingship of Jesus, who offers us freedom by His sacrificial death on the cross.*

---

Sadly, no king of Israel was ever able to meet God's requirements fully. Even King David, who is widely regarded as Israel's best king, committed terrible acts of sin. As the years wore on and Israel's earthly kings failed to live up to God's instructions time and time again, the people desired a true and better King to come—a descendent of Abraham who would perfectly reign.

Thankfully, this perfect King came in the Son of God, Jesus Christ. Fully God and fully man, Jesus left His throne in heaven to live on earth and fulfill all the requirements for kingship. He was sent by God the Father and obedient to God's every command. He is from the line of Judah (Genesis 49:10)—one of God's chosen people. Rather than a palace, baby Jesus was placed into a lowly manger. In His time on earth, He amassed no great wealth, no vast army, or no noble family but instead lived by modest means. The Israelites desired a political leader with military prowess (1 Samuel 8:20) so that they could be like other nations. But Jesus came not to deliver His people from earthly enemies but to deliver them from sin. He came to earth not to be served but to serve us all by giving up His life on the cross so that we may be forgiven (Mark 10:45).

Jesus is the perfect embodiment of kingship. He uses His power to serve and save, and He invites us into His eternal kingdom. In this life, we must choose which king we will serve. Either we live under the kingship of the enemy, an oppressive ruler who enslaves us to sin, or we live under the kingship of Jesus, who offers us freedom by His sacrificial death on the cross. Which will we choose?

QUESTIONS

**1** How are the requirements for kingship in Deuteronomy different from the requirements for leadership in our modern-day governments and jobs?

QUESTIONS CONTINUE ▶

**2** Why is leadership important in our lives? How do you most often respond to God's leadership?

**3** What do you put your trust in rather than trusting in God's provision?

## Notes

Jesus was born into this world to become the leader of God's people.

# The Rejection of the King

**READ JUDGES 2, I SAMUEL 8:6 – 21**

Rejection is a sharp blade capable of cutting to the deepest parts of us. You may have faced rejection in the form of a college you did not get into, a friend group that would not accept you, or a significant other who ended a relationship. The pain that comes after rejection is quick, yet the wound from it can last for years. And some of the most biting rejection comes when we offer to help someone who refuses our aid. We watch helplessly as they fall deeper into their pain but will not allow anyone to pull them out of it. In a similar way, time and time again, God sees His people fall into sin yet refuse to repent and return to Him for help.

After leading His people out of Egypt and through the wilderness, God gave Israel the Promised Land and commanded them to rely only on Him to protect and provide for them in it. God would be the King over this nation, and He would rule with justice, mercy, kindness, and power. This trust in God alone meant the Israelites could not make covenants with other nations for protection or worship other gods, or there would be consequences. Just as in today's world, where there are laws to ensure justice and punishments when those laws are broken, God created laws to ensure Israel's faithfulness and curses if Israel broke their promises to Him (Deuteronomy 28).

All of God's laws are good because He is good, and He will hold His people accountable because He is just. This is the kind of king we want. We want a king who creates laws for the good of us and our nation, and we want a king who upholds those laws to ensure justice.

---

*We have a King who will never leave us and who sacrifices Himself to set His people free. Let all the citizens of God's kingdom celebrate His perfect, eternal, and just rule this Christmas season.*

---

However, Israel failed to keep their promises to God. Rather than trusting God to provide, they served the supposed gods of the storms, rain, love, and fertility to make sure they had agricultural success. We often do the same thing. We put our eggs in all the baskets we can. We pray to God but also work on our own to achieve what we want; we trust in God to provide but also stress over building up enough savings in case He does not; we know God made us and loves us but try to change everything we can about ourselves so that others will accept us. We cannot serve two kings. We are either citizens of one kingdom or enemies of it. While Israel still obeyed some of God's law, they ultimately rejected God as King by failing to serve Him alone. While Israel appeared to serve God and idols at the same time, in reality, they were actually rejecting God as King as they served false gods.

When most of us are rejected, we put as much distance between that person and us as possible. God, however, refuses to run from His people. He is not a ruler who locks the guilty in jail and throws away the key—He is One who offers mercy instead. He sent judges to lead the people back to His laws and the peace and joy that come from following them. When these good leaders ruled, the people thrived. Once they died, however, Israel returned to their treacherous ways. Over the years of the rule of the judges, Israel fell deeper into sin and betrayal of their King. By the time of the last judge, Samuel, Israel completely rejected God as King and demanded a human king to rule over them instead.

The more Israel trusted in the things of this world, the less they trusted in God's power. They abandoned the King who freed them from slavery in Egypt to once again enslave themselves to a human king who would take their children, crops, and animals to build up his own palace. Like Israel, we would rather bow to idols than God. We serve the things of this world that we think will provide us with success, comfort, and protection because we do not trust God to give us the things we need. We choose the rulers of this world over the King of heaven and earth. Because God is just, there are consequences when we betray His kingship. We all deserve death as a punishment for our treachery against Him (Romans 6:23).

Like Israel, we need a good ruler who can guide us back to God. Jesus was born into this world to become the leader of God's people. He lived in perfect obedience to God, showing us the path back into a relationship with our true King. He, too, was rejected by us and died under a mocking sign that read, "King of the Jews" (Matthew 27:37, Luke 23:38, John 19:19). Unlike the other leaders, though, Jesus did not stay in the grave, leaving us without a leader. He came back to life—eternal life—to reign over the kingdom of God. In doing so, Jesus freed us from the punishment of our betrayal by dying in our place on the cross. God forgives our sin because it has been paid for on the cross. Jesus's death shows us God's justice, mercy, and love all at once. We have a King who will never leave us and who sacrifices Himself to set His people free. Let all the citizens of God's kingdom celebrate His perfect, eternal, and just rule this Christmas season.

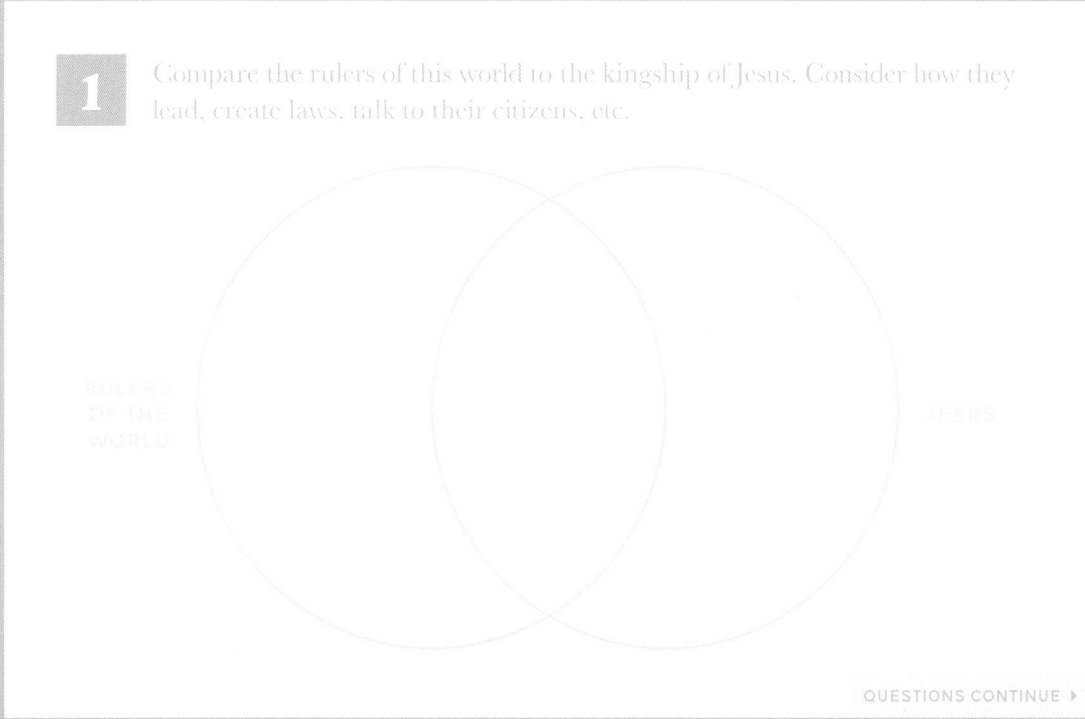

**QUESTIONS**

**1** Compare the rulers of this world to the kingship of Jesus. Consider how they lead, create laws, talk to their citizens, etc.

RULERS OF THE WORLD

JESUS

QUESTIONS CONTINUE ▶

**2** Why would Israel reject God as King?

**3** How can you embrace God's authority rather than rejecting it?

## Notes

Jesus's birth fulfilled the prophecies God gave His people.

# The Anticipated King

**READ ISAIAH 9:1–7, MICAH 5:1–6**

You awaken on Christmas morning to a pile of presents under the tree, and an enormous box covered in shiny wrapping paper catches your eye. You rush toward it and squeal in excitement because your name is written plainly on the top. You start to imagine what could be inside, hoping it is the toy you have begged for all year long. The anticipation mounts as you await your turn to open a gift, but when you rip off the paper, you find that it is not a toy like what you expected it to be but a book. You are disappointed because it is not what you anticipated.

This is what the Israelites experienced when waiting for the Messiah. For thousands of years, God's people looked to the heavens, wondering when He would arrive. Day after day, year after year, century after century, they waited. Where was this promised king to free them from oppression and corruption? When would the reign of peace and joy begin? They believed that this king would come and free them from the foreign rule that plagued them for centuries and restore Israel to the kingdom it had been so long before. Indeed, the King was coming, but He would not be what anyone expected.

After rejecting God's rule, God gave His people what they wanted—a human king named Saul. Although Saul led Israel well at first, he became ensnared in his own pursuit of glory over obedience to God and service of the people. The very thing that God warned Israel about came true. Because of Saul's disobedience, God replaced Saul with a new king named David.

David ruled Israel well and led them into a golden age of spiritual, economic, and military success. However, like all leaders before him, David died. The throne was passed to his son Solomon, who was wise, rich, and powerful. He was the very picture of what we likely imagine a king should be. However, Solomon also fell into the pit of selfish desires—he enslaved his own people in order to build up his kingdom and married foreign wives who led him away from God. Solomon's disobedience led to the disobedience of all of Israel (1 Kings 11:29–37), resulting in the nation of Israel splitting into two nations: the nation of Israel to the north and the nation of Judah to the south.

Israel and Judah both rode roller coasters of dynasties for decades, with some kings faithfully following God, resulting in the nation following Him as well, but other evil kings who led themselves and Israel away from their Creator. God continually sent prophets to beg the kings and people to return to Him, but each time, the people failed to do so long-term. After generations of disobedience, God allowed His people to be conquered by foreign armies, ending the reign of Israel and Judah's kings.

Even though the kings and people constantly turned away from God, He still offered them hope. The prophet Isaiah warned Israel of the imminent conquest of Assyria because of their rejection of God. As Isaiah painted a bleak picture of Israel's future, he also promised them that one day a new King would arise. This King will shine light into the darkest of nights, and He will break the rod of oppression that has held the people in bondage.

*The Prince of Peace has arrived and will reign on earth in the hearts of all who receive Him.*

Unlike Saul and Solomon, this King is born for us (Luke 2:11). He will serve the people under His rule rather than command their service. This King will be a Prince of Peace, bringing rest and satisfaction to His kingdom. He will be a Wonderful Counselor full of wisdom to offer His people (Isaiah 9:6). And strangely, the prophet Micah tells us that He will come from a small, often-forgotten town called Bethlehem. This King will not be tucked away in a castle but exposed to us all. He will not be isolated from us but given for us. He will serve the lowly and forgotten rather than bow down to the rich and proud.

Isaiah prophesied this King would come from the line of David and reign forever. God's people heard this and imagined this new King would come just like David, a handsome and strong warrior who led a powerful army. They expected Him to overthrow their oppressor and reestablish a kingdom of Israel that would be as powerful as the nation under David. For hundreds of years, the Israelites waited for this

King to appear. However, when He arrived, the people were confused.

This King was not handsome, powerful, or a military leader. Instead, He was a humble carpenter from Nazareth, a town that people did not expect anything good to come from (John 1:46). Jesus is not the King the people expected because He is so much more. The rulers of the world ultimately serve themselves. They use their appearances, power, and wealth to control others. Yet Jesus establishes a new kingdom where the King lays down His life for His people. Jesus did not come to rule over a piece of land but over the hearts of those who choose Him. He brings freedom from oppression, not by overthrowing governments but by freeing us from the burden of sin. Jesus is the greatest gift the world will ever receive, even if He came in a package no one would have expected.

Jesus's birth fulfilled the prophecies God gave His people. Just like David, Jesus ushers in a golden age for all who follow Him. It is not a golden age of wealth and power, but for those in His kingdom, it is one of joy and peace that starts now and lasts into eternity. The Prince of Peace has arrived and will reign on earth in the hearts of all who receive Him. The wait for the King is over. Jesus is here.

QUESTIONS

1    How did Jesus fulfill the prophecies of Isaiah and Micah?

QUESTIONS CONTINUE ▶

**2** What is the danger of putting our trust in human leaders?

**3** Do you feel like you are living in a golden age under the rule of Jesus? Why or why not?

**Notes**

# VERSE MAP

There are many ways to digest God's Word. You can read it silently, aloud, or with others, or you can even have the Bible read to you. You can read entire chapters or books of the Bible at a time or go verse by verse. One way to study Scripture deeply is to create a verse map. This process allows you to dig into the meaning of one or two verses at a time so that you can better understand the meaning and, thus, have greater intimacy with God.

The following analogy can best describe the process of verse mapping: Imagine looking at a great forest. From far away, you see thousands of trees that all look nearly identical. As you walk closer, you start to notice the subtle differences between each tree. Then, you stare closely at just one tree and notice each knot and leaf. Verse mapping allows you to look at just one passage in a forest of Scripture so that you can notice it for its unique beauty. Look at the verse map below for Philippians 2:9.

The goal of a verse map is to understand what the passage means and how it applies to our lives. To do this, you must research the passage by reading multiple translations, looking up cross-references (comparing this verse to other verses on the same subject), turning to trusted commentaries, and understanding grammar and sentence structure. This process may seem daunting at first, but take it one step at a time, and you might soon find the joy of studying God's Word through a verse map.

# Philippians 2:9

BECAUSE JESUS OBEYED GOD BY LEAVING HEAVEN AND DYING ON THE CROSS (VERSES 7-8) ←

FOR THIS REASON

ELEVATED (NLT)

GOD HIGHLY EXALTED HIM → JESUS

AND GAVE HIM THE NAME

THAT IS ABOVE EVERY NAME

↓

JESUS IS GREATER THAN ALL

## ON THE NEXT PAGE, YOU WILL CREATE A VERSE MAP FOR PHILIPPIANS 2:10–11.

**1.** Pray for understanding.

**2.** Read the passage carefully in multiple translations. You can find these on a Bible app or the internet. Write down any differences you see.

**3.** Notice the grammar and sentence structure. What verb tense is used? Are there any repeated words or phrases? What conjunctions (e.g., if, but, and) are there? Circle or underline anything that stands out to you.

**4.** Look at the context. What is happening before and after this passage that helps you understand the meaning?

**5.** Look at a commentary of this passage if you have one.

**6.** Apply. Ask yourself these three questions.

- What attribute of God do I notice in this passage?

- What do I learn about myself in light of God from this passage?

- How should this passage change the way I think, speak, or act?

NOTES

# Philippians 2:10–11

SO THAT AT THE NAME OF JESUS

EVERY KNEE WILL BOW —

IN HEAVEN AND ON EARTH

AND UNDER THE EARTH —

AND EVERY TONGUE WILL CONFESS

THAT JESUS CHRIST IS LORD,

TO THE GLORY OF GOD THE FATHER.

All the world will
know who the true
King of kings is.

POST CARD

# Jesus: The King of Kings

**READ MATTHEW 2:1–12, PHILIPPIANS 2:9–11, REVELATION 19:11–16**

History remembers monarchs as beloved or evil. We assign them titles such as Catherine the Great, Ivan the Terrible, and Mad King George III. In reality, almost every past king possessed both admirable and abhorrent qualities. They were each loved by some and hated by others. In this Advent season, we await the coming of not just a king but the King of kings. This is the ruler who places all other rulers on their thrones, the only King who can truthfully be called "great" because there is no bad quality within Him.

Israel had been waiting for centuries for this promised King to appear. Yet when He came, He was rejected by His people just as His Father had been. Instead of God's people bowing before their long-awaited monarch, a group of foreign men from the east made their way to His side. Little is known about these men. Some call them the Magi, coming from the Greek word *magos*, which can denote someone from a priestly lineage, a sorcerer, or one who studies astronomy or dreams. In any case, these men follow a star in order to meet someone of great importance.

While Israel ignored the arrival of Jesus, the wise men traveled far for months or perhaps even years to celebrate

Him. They went to Jerusalem to see this new-born King. At the time, Jerusalem was the seat of political and economic power in the area, making it the obvious location for a king to reside. The men entered the palace in Jerusalem but were surprised when they were told that the King they were searching for was not there but in a small town called Bethlehem. They then left the palace and headed toward a home far away from grandeur. The moment they set their eyes on this child monarch, they bowed down and worshiped, offering Him the finest gifts. It is important to note that the first people to bow to Jesus as King were not Jews but Gentiles. Jesus came to fulfill the promises of God to be the King of the Jews, but He did not stop there. Breaking heaven's doors open, Jesus announced Himself as King and Savior to all—Gentiles and Jews.

---

*Breaking heaven's doors open, Jesus announced Himself as King and Savior to all — Gentiles and Jews.*

---

But not everyone was so excited about this new ruler. Herod was afraid of this young boy. Herod was the king of the Jews at this time in history, and he ruled under the authority of the Roman Empire. He fought his way to his seat of power and refused to allow it to be taken. Rather than bow down to another, Herod chose murder

(Matthew 1:16–18). Even the rest of the scribes and scholars of Jerusalem who told the wise men where to find this boy stayed put in their homes rather than traveling the mere five miles between the two cities to see Him. By ignoring His presence, they rejected His kingship. We all react to the reign of Jesus. Either we rejoice that He rules over the world with justice and mercy, as the wise men did, or we rebel against His reign and try to keep all power for ourselves, as the rulers in Jerusalem did.

Although Jesus came to this earth quietly in humble circumstances and died a criminal's death on the cross, He now sits on an eternal throne in heaven. This suffering servant is now an exalted King. One day, Jesus will return to earth much differently than the way He first arrived. This second coming will not be mild and gentle but stunning and magnificent. The world will see Jesus as the true glorified King He is when He descends from heaven with an angelic army following behind. All nations will crumble before Him as the world sees His power is greater than any other. At this second coming, all of the enemies of God's kingdom will finally fall. Death, disease, hatred, corruption, shame, lust, and greed will evaporate like the morning dew as the sun shines upon it.

The reign of Jesus is not waiting on His second coming, however. It is already here. Jesus inaugurated His kingdom with His life, death, and resurrection. Dying for us, He opened a pathway into citizenship where we can find freedom. Unlike other kingdoms where one is born into citizenship, entry into the kingdom of God is by choice. God's people are not from one region of the world or one people group. God's kingdom is unbound by ethnicity, race, or land boundary. None of us are initially born into it, but we can all be reborn as citizens of it when we accept the kingship of Jesus over our lives and the entire universe.

One day, Jesus will return to earth not as a baby but as a Warrior King. At that time, every knee will bow, just as the wise men did in His presence. All the world will know who the true King of kings is. In this season of celebration, let us praise God not only because Jesus came to the world two thousand years ago but also for the truth that He is coming again to rule over a new heaven and new earth as the King forevermore.

QUESTIONS

**1** Why is Jesus the King of kings?

QUESTIONS CONTINUE ▶

**2** Compare the first coming of Jesus that we celebrate on Christmas to His second coming that is described in the book of Revelation.

FIRST COMING | SECOND COMING

**3** How does the description of Jesus in Revelation change the way you view Him?

134

**Notes**

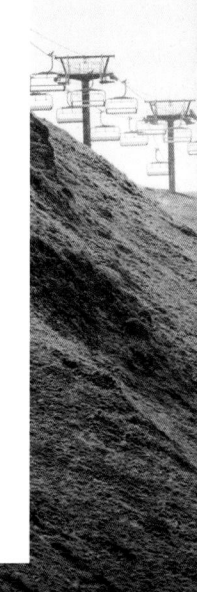

The kingdom of God is
eternal and will never fall.

# Jesus: The Kingdom of Christ

READ JOHN 18:36, EPHESIANS 1:20–22, EPHESIANS 2:6

Whenever a major military battle was won, the ancient Romans held a triumph in the city. The victorious general, dressed in purple and gold and holding a scepter, rode through the streets in a laurel-laden chariot. This victor stood high above the crowd, looking down on them from his seat of power and prestige as a slave held a golden crown above his head. Great political leaders, musicians, sacrificial animals, and treasures from war all preceded this military leader in a parade that culminated in a great feast of celebration. But this triumph of glory only occurred after a great battle was waged and won.

Jesus fought the greatest battle in history against sin and death on the cross. Rather than conquering an emperor, He sacrificed for the people. This battle took all that Jesus physically had. He was beaten, lashed, humiliated, and tortured to death. But three days later, He rose again in victory. Jesus died a criminal's death but is now raised as royalty.

After Christ accomplished His redemptive work on the cross and rose from the grave, He went back to heaven as a victorious King. High above all the rulers of the earth,

Jesus sits on a heavenly throne in power and glory at the right hand of God the Father. This is the position of greatest honor, showing the respect and love the Father has for His Son. All heavenly creatures bow down to Him as voices cry out His powerful name. Yet the kingdom of God is not isolated to heaven but has crashed into our world.

As previously discussed, shortly before Jesus began His three-year ministry, His cousin John the Baptist began preaching for the people to "repent, because the kingdom of heaven has come near" (Matthew 3:2). The King of heaven came down to earth, not to restore the long-gone kingdom of Israel but to create a new Messianic kingdom that had been promised to David so many years before.

This kingdom would prove far greater than the kingdom of Israel. It is not bound to one piece of land but covers the planet. It is not designated for one people group, but all believers, whether Jews or Gentiles, are welcomed as citizens. It is not bound by time but will last forever. This kingdom appears invisible to many but becomes more and more apparent to the world through God's people, the Church.

Jesus reigns over all the earth, and the reality of His heavenly kingdom is revealed through the Church. It is not great pastors, programs, or people that make the Church great—it is our powerful King. Jesus is the head of the Church, bringing more into its fold and guiding it with His Word. The kingdom begins in each of our hearts when we recognize the power of Jesus to save us from our sins and choose to enter into His kingdom. We then reveal His kingdom to the world as we live alongside other kingdom-minded people in the Church.

You are not the only subject of Jesus; you are one of many. We must live united with the whole kingdom of God here on earth to protect ourselves against the schemes of the enemy and show the lost where they might be found. We reveal God's kingdom as we live as its subjects. We obey and follow Jesus with our whole lives, showing that He is truly our King. His laws are the foundation of our community within the Church and our families. His promises are the hope we rest in. He is our ultimate authority.

*Jesus reigns over all the earth, and the reality of His heavenly kingdom is revealed through the Church.*

Jesus is the One we bow before and the One to whom we owe our deepest allegiance. We recognize His ultimate authority above the lesser authorities of nations, political parties, or famous teachers. In this kingdom, we are not just ruled by a King, but we are one with Him. Just as two become one in marriage, we become one with Christ when we are saved. We are buried with Him in the ground and raised to new eternal life with Him as well. The Church, as the community of believers, has the power of Christ to help us live in obedience and proclaim the gospel to the nations. We are co-heirs to the kingdom of God alongside Jesus.

The kingdom of God is not like the kingdoms created in this world. The great and powerful Roman empire that paraded their victorious leaders and crucified Jesus is now nothing more than ruins. All empires fall, and all rulers meet the same fate—death. But the kingdom of God is in this world and yet stretches beyond it. It is eternal and will never fall. And its King, Jesus, defeated death and now sits on His throne forever. This is a King we can trust and a kingdom in which we can put our hope.

While Jesus inaugurated the kingdom of heaven in His earthly ministry, it will be fully consummated when He comes again. Heaven and earth will collide under the glorious rule of King Jesus, who will return to earth to fully eradicate death and sin. Until that glorious day, let all members of the Messianic kingdom live in loving obedience to our King and wait in hope for His triumphant return.

QUESTIONS

**1** How can you live like a citizen of the kingdom of God?

QUESTIONS CONTINUE ▶

**2** Why do we need to be active participants in the Church?

**3** How do these passages change the way you view the role of the Church in God's kingdom?

# APPLICATION

*Before we begin a new week of study, take some time to apply and share the truths of Scripture you learned this week. Here are a few ideas of how you could do this:*

- Schedule a meet-up with a friend to share what you are learning from God's Word.

- Use these prompts to journal or pray through what God is revealing to you through your study of His Word.

  *Lord, I feel…*

  *Lord, You are…*

  *Lord, forgive me for…*

*Lord, help me with…*

- Spend time worshiping God in a way that is meaningful to you, whether that is taking a walk in nature, painting, drawing, singing, etc.

- Paraphrase the Scripture you read this week.

- Use a study Bible or commentary to help you answer questions that came up as you read this week's Scripture.

- Use highlighters to mark the places you see the metanarrative of Scripture in one or more of the passages of Scripture that you read this week. (See The Metanarrative of Scripture on page 174.)

# Messiah

✝

JESUS CHRIST IS THE MESSIAH

WHO LOVES US SO MUCH

HE CAME TO SAVE US.

*Candle Lighting*

# Love

NOTE: TO BE COMPLETED
TOGETHER WITH "WHO
IS THE MESSIAH?"

4 · 1

Today, we light the love candle. As we light the love candle, we can remember that Jesus is our Messiah and that He gave His life out of God's great love for us.

### FATHER,

Thank You for loving us so much that You sent Your Son to take on our sins, die a sinner's death, and be raised to life three days later so that we can have eternal life with You. Father, we confess that we do not always love others in the way that You love us. We pray that we can better know Your love so that we can love You and others well. We pray that Your Spirit continues to make us Christlike so that people may see Your Son in us.

### WE PRAY THIS IN YOUR SON'S PRECIOUS NAME,

### AMEN

# Memory
# Verse

4 · 1

For a child will be born for us,
a son will be given to us, and
the government will be on his
shoulders. He will be named
Wonderful Counselor, Mighty God,
Eternal Father, Prince of Peace.

ISAIAH 9:6

The Messiah has come.

# Who Is the Messiah?

**READ I SAMUEL 10:1, I SAMUEL 16:13, LUKE 2:8–20**

Winds rustle the grasses of the countryside in Israel. The night is quiet and still—much like every other night. Stars shine above while a group of shepherds faithfully tend to their flock. Little do they know, this night is not normal. This night will change the trajectory of not only their lives but of all human history. A bright light pierces the darkness, and the shepherds cower in fear. An angel of the Lord stands before them, sharing good news of great joy. The long-awaited Messiah has finally been born! Immediately, these shepherds leave their flocks on this hillside and venture toward Bethlehem, abandoning everything to lay eyes on this baby boy (Luke 2:8–20).

Why the haste? Why were these shepherds so desperate to meet this child?

Marked by oppression, poor leadership, and hearts prone to wandering, God's chosen people longed for a breath under wave after wave of hardship. This breath—this hope—is the Messiah. From moments after the Fall of Man in Genesis 3, God promised a Savior to finally end sin's grip on the world (Genesis 3:15). He promised a Messiah who would end oppression and break the chains of slavery for Israel. This Messiah would conquer enemies in God's name and eventually restore Israel to its promised glory. God's children would finally claim victory.

The hope of the Messiah passed down from generation to generation. Israel saw the kings of neighboring nations and begged God for one of their own. God granted their wish and chose Saul, handsome and a head taller than most, to be king of Israel. In 1 Samuel 10:1, Samuel, a faithful priest of the time, anointed and commissioned Saul, declaring him ruler of God's people.

In ancient Israel, priests and kings were anointed with olive oil to symbolize being chosen by God. These men were set apart for God's good works, responsible for guiding and leading Israel in obedience to the Lord. In fact, Messiah means "anointed one" or "chosen one." And so, with each anointing, Israel wondered, *Is this our Messiah?*

---

◆

## At the birth of Christ, the Scriptures began to illuminate. God's promises were proven true.

---

Sadly, Saul failed to obey God. The Lord removed His Spirit from Saul and instead chose David to reign over His people. We see David's anointing in 1 Samuel 16:13. Scripture tells us that God's Spirit came powerfully on David and even calls David a man after God's own heart (1 Samuel 13:14, Acts 13:22). In many ways,

David fit the description of the Messiah. He defeated surrounding nations in God's name. Wealth and prosperity flowed into Israel. God's nation was feared by surrounding peoples. David sought the Lord's guidance in decisions. But, though David loved God, he was a sinner, just like us. David's leadership spiraled out of control when he slept with Bathsheba and had her husband, Uriah, killed to cover up his mistake (2 Samuel 11). Though David is regarded as one of Israel's best kings, he was a mere shadow of the true and faithful King to come. Israel again was left waiting for their Messiah.

King after king was anointed to rule over Israel in the coming years. With each new king, Israel asked, "Is this our Messiah?" None of these kings proved worthy of the title. In the waiting, Israel often turned their heads away from God and toward gods of surrounding nations, hoping to somehow dig themselves out of oppression by their own strength. Even in the midst of Israel's unfaithfulness, God never removed His promise for future redemption. Our gracious Father still kept His plan intact, working in even the most despairing circumstances for Israel's good and His glory.

The Messiah meant great hope and great joy for Israel, so much so that on the night of His birth, the shepherds ran through fields just to be in His presence. Scripture does not tell us that the shepherds took time to secure provision for their sheep or update their families on their whereabouts. Instead, they moved in haste to see hope fulfilled. Scripture tells us that these shepherds left the Messiah's presence glorifying and praising God, sharing the good news with anyone they met. The deep breath of redemption finally came to Israel.

As we look forward to Christmas Day, we can find a deeper reverence for this baby in a manger who we celebrate. We are reminded of the cries of God's children and the countless prayers lifted in longing—all dreaming of the day their Messiah would arrive. Second Corinthians 1:20 reads, "For every one of God's promises is 'Yes' in him. Therefore, through him we also say 'Amen' to the glory of God." At the birth of Christ, the Scriptures began to illuminate. God's promises were proven true. Years of waiting and wondering were now tenderly answered by the coos of a newborn boy. Though hope was thought to be lost, now, it is found. The Messiah has come.

# QUESTIONS

**1** Even after the Fall of man and the continuous disobedience of Israel, God still kept His promise to provide a Messiah. What does this tell us about God's character?

QUESTIONS CONTINUE ▶

**2** How did Israel's history impact their desire for a Messiah?

**3** Think about a time when you waited upon God. What did you learn from that season?

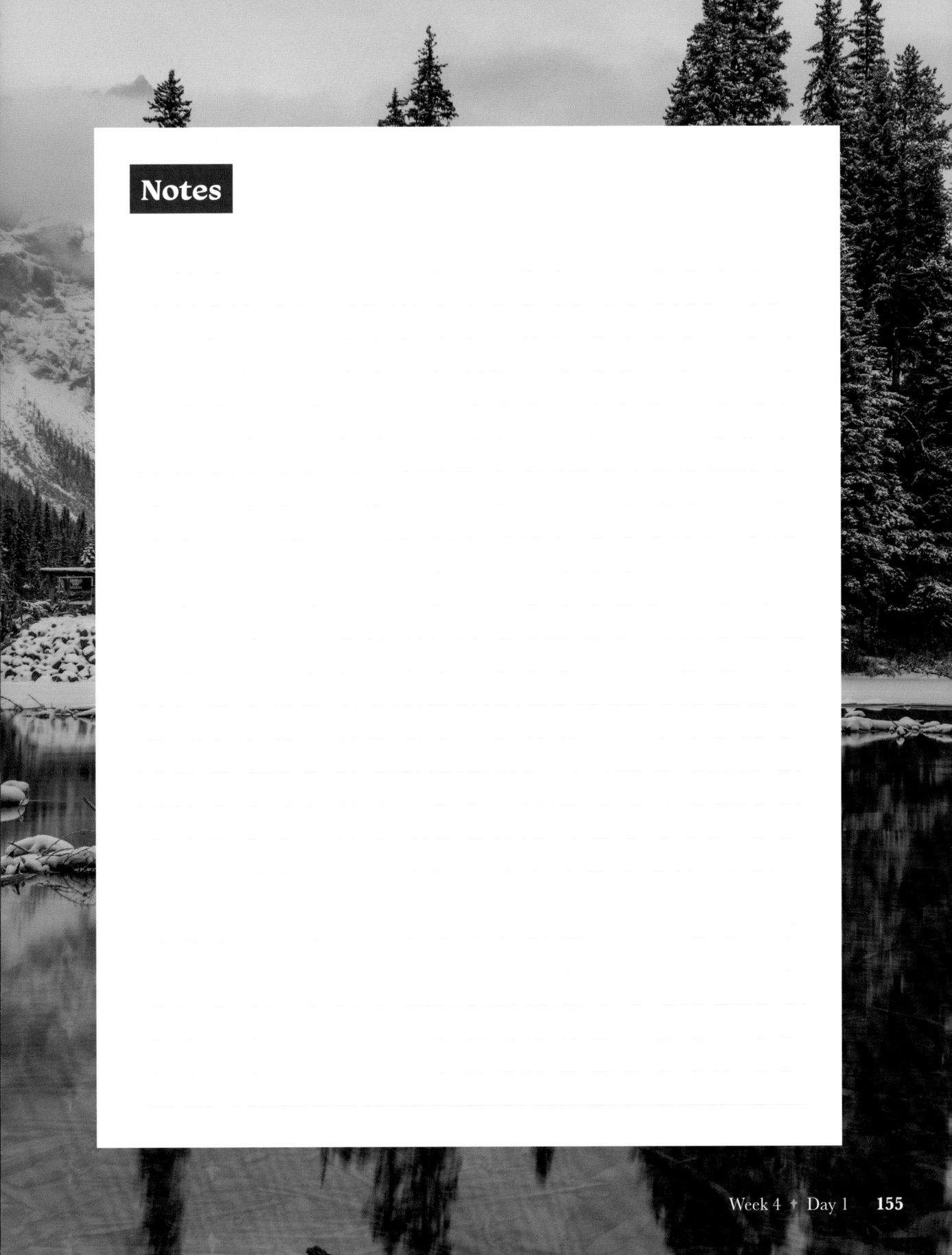

## Notes

# Christ Candle

NOTE: TO BE COMPLETED
TOGETHER WITH "JESUS:
THE MESSIAH IS HERE!"

4 · 2

PECKSNIFF'S

AROMATHERAPY
RE-CHARGE
FRAGRANCED CA...

Today, we light the Christ candle. As we light the Christ candle, we thank God for sending His perfect Son, who is the perfect Prophet, Priest, King, and Messiah, so that we can have eternal life with Him.

### FATHER,

Today is the day we celebrate the birth that changed everything. We praise You that You are a faithful God who always fulfills His promises, even when we are unfaithful to You. Thank You for loving us so much that You sent Your one and only Son to walk this earth, to sympathize with us, and to die on the cross in our place so that we can approach Your throne with boldness. We love You. May You be praised forever and ever.

### WE PRAY THIS IN YOUR SON'S PRECIOUS NAME,

### AMEN

Jesus has come once, and He will come again.

# Jesus: The Messiah Is Here!

**READ LUKE 2:19, REVELATION 11:15**

Do you have a favorite Christmas memory? Maybe your mind immediately goes to a gift from childhood that brings you joy. Maybe you can hear the laugh of a lost loved one. Or maybe you smell your mother's Christmas dinner. No doubt, Mary held onto Jesus's birth story in a similar way. Luke 2:19 reads, "But Mary was treasuring up all these things in her heart and meditating on them." Surely, years later, she could still smell the musty scent of the manger, hear Jesus's coos, and feel His little hand grip her fingers. Did Jesus radiate with hope as a newborn? Was there anything different about His cries? Were His eyes deep with compassion from the very beginning? This verse prompts us to pause and put ourselves in Mary's shoes. In her arms, she held the culmination of prayers answered and promises fulfilled. This boy was *God incarnate* and everything she—and her people—had been waiting for. This newborn baby Mary comforted was the final Prophet, the Great High Priest, the everlasting King, and the long-anticipated Messiah.

As we snuggle by the Christmas tree, sipping our coffee and relishing in this joyous season, let us reflect on what we have learned through these weeks of expanding our reverence of Jesus.

Jesus is the final Prophet—the only One who could perfectly communicate on behalf of God. He had no need to interpret visions or tell of a coming Savior. He is the dream that became a reality, the truth-teller with the very mind of God. Jesus is the Word of God. He invites us to know hope.

Jesus is the Great High Priest—the only One who sacrificed Himself on behalf of the people. He was the spotless Lamb whose sinless blood covered the sins of all humanity. Jesus tore down the dividing wall of hostility (Ephesians 2:14) and invited us into the Holy of Holies. Without fear or doubt, we can come near to the throne of God. He invites us to know peace.

Jesus is the everlasting King—the only One whose kingdom knows no end. He is the leader we long to follow, who executes perfect justice and rules in full wisdom. He is the compassionate ruler, the friend of the outcast, the One who elevates the poor and rewards the righteous. His kingdom is not threatened or shaken. Under His rule, our days are marked by endless praise. He invites us to know joy.

Jesus is the long-anticipated Messiah—the Chosen One in whom Israel placed their hope. He is the fulfillment of past promises and the confidence of our future. He is David's rightful heir. He is the heart of God in flesh. He is the hand of God—embracing His children, healing wounds, and dining in the presence of man. He invites us to know love.

Like Mary, take the time to treasure and meditate on these truths in your heart. Do you need hope? Do you long for peace? Do you thirst for joy again? Do you need to know you are deeply loved? In Christ, we discover the answers to our questions. We find our hunger appeased and our longings satiated. He is, in fact, everything we need.

And yet, like the Israelites waited for the Messiah, we, too, wait for His glorious return. Revelation 11:15 (NIV) proclaims, "The kingdom of the world has become the kingdom of our Lord and of his Messiah, and he will reign forever and ever." Our hearts long for this day—when Jesus will finally bring heaven to earth; when tears, pain, and suffering will be no more; when we can finally rest in the presence of our Savior. We know all too well the sting of sin, and we see brokenness on display in the world around us. Even Christmastime is marred by the Fall. We mourn unmet expectations, familial disagreements, plans that go awry, and loved ones who are no longer with us. At Christmas, we celebrate but also grieve a world that desperately needs Jesus's return.

What is the difference between our waiting and the Israelites' waiting? We know Jesus came as a little baby in Bethlehem, sinless, humble, yet all-powerful. We know that He grew to perfectly serve God, healing and teaching along the way. We know He died a gruesome death on the cross, bearing the weight of our sins on His shoulders. We know He rose three days later, conquering the enemy and establishing full victory over death. We see the promises fulfilled. Jesus has come once, and He will come again. This time, we wait in confidence.

This waiting is not passive. We do not sit on our couches and continually watch our clocks for Jesus's return. No, this waiting is active. We have a job to do—a treasure to share. Throughout this study, we have seen Jesus prove Himself to be worthy over and over again. He is the Light of the World, the light that darkness will never overcome (John 1:5). Our broken bodies are the very vessels He chose to share this hope with the world (2 Corinthians 4:7–10). As we celebrate Christmas Day, may our hands and our lips praise Him. May we mourn with those whose Christmas may be painful. May we wash the dishes after Christmas dinner without grumbling. May we share the true gift of Jesus as we unwrap presents. May we let this renewed reverence of King Jesus, the Messiah, the final Prophet, and our Great High Priest deepen our joy.

The truth is, we will spend eternity growing in awe and wonder of our Savior—and it will never be enough. Let us again put ourselves in Mary's shoes, captivated by the glory of the newborn Messiah in her arms. Perhaps Mary knew these memories of Jesus's boyhood were worth more than gold. Perhaps, through her stories, the authors of the Gospels recounted Jesus's birth. Perhaps she knew coming generations needed these details of the humble beginnings of the King of kings. Jesus is worth more than any celebration we could throw, any words we could utter, any song we could sing. He is worthy of our hearts, our motivations, our time, and our resources. Jesus is worthy of our attention this Christmas and for all of our days forevermore.

# QUESTIONS

**1** Reflect on the four roles of Christ studied this Advent season. What hope do they bring you today?

PROPHET

PRIEST

KING

MESSIAH

QUESTIONS CONTINUE ▶

**2** Why can we have joy as we wait for Christ's return?

**3** Consider Luke 2:19. Is treasuring Jesus a regular habit of yours? How can you continue or begin to treasure Jesus in your life?

# Notes

# WORD STUDY

## Christos Χριστός

Greek for "anointed one," "Christ," or "Messiah"

Found in the New Testament 569 times

## mās̆aḥ

Hebrew for "anoint"

Root of the word "Messiah"

Occurs in the Old Testament 69 times

Did you know that "Messiah" and "Christ" are synonyms—two words that mean the same thing? The Old Testament, written primarily in Hebrew, uses the word *Mās̆aḥ* to describe anointing. This is where the word "Messiah" finds its origin. "Messiah" means "anointed one" or "chosen one," and this word was often used to describe a priest or king who was chosen by God to lead His people. An anointing was a special ritual performed at the beginning of one's service or reign, in which the anointed was covered with oil to symbolize being set apart by God. Often the Spirit of God then rested uniquely with the leader. In ancient Israel, "Messiah" held the weight of Israel's future on its shoulders. God promised to send a future Anointed One who would take away the sins of the world, conquer their enemies, and establish a kingdom that would never end.

The New Testament, written in Greek, translates "Anointed One" as "christos." In fact, Christ and Messiah are often used interchangeably between modern translations of the Bible, all with the root word "christos." "Christos" is referenced in the New Testament 569 times. The repetition of this word highlights a major theme of the Gospels and the entire New Testament—that Jesus is indeed the fulfillment of the prophecies of old. When we pray in reverence to Jesus Christ, we are, in fact, proclaiming that He is the beloved Chosen One of God, sent to redeem His people from slavery to sin and free them into His coming kingdom. The term "Christ" is rich with meaning, serving as a bridge that connects the promises and anticipation of the Old Testament with the hope fulfilled in the New Testament.

## Māšaḥ in the Old Testament

*Exodus 40:13*

Clothe Aaron with the holy garments, anoint him, and consecrate him, so that he can serve me as a priest.

*1 Samuel 9:16*

At this time tomorrow I will send you a man from the land of Benjamin. Anoint him ruler over my people Israel. He will save them from the Philistines because I have seen the affliction of my people, for their cry has come to me.

## Christos in the New Testament

*Luke 9:20*

"But you," he asked them, "who do you say that I am?"

Peter answered, "God's Messiah."

*John 4:25*

The woman said to him, "I know that the Messiah is coming" (who is called Christ). "When he comes, he will explain everything to us."

*John 17:3*

This is eternal life: that they may know you, the only true God, and the one you have sent—Jesus Christ.

## ATONEMENT

**1.** When the high priest would offer a sacrifice to God in order to cover Israel's sins and restore their relationship with God. **2.** The restoration of our relationship with God through Jesus's sacrifice on the cross, which, by grace, covered our sins and made a way for our forgiveness.

## CONSECRATED

To be regarded as holy and set apart. Priests in the Old Testament were consecrated for their service to God in the temple. In Christ, all believers are consecrated by the blood of Christ, for it is Christ's blood that makes believers pure.

## COVENANT

A binding agreement between two parties by which each party commits to fulfill certain conditions and receives certain benefits. When we speak about God's covenant generally, we refer to God's covenant that He made primarily with the people of Israel. These were promises to form the Israelites into one nation, bless them, give them a land to call their own, and deliver them through a promised Savior. But God also formed covenants associated with these blessings with Noah, Abraham, Moses, and David, and all of these covenants have been fulfilled through Christ.

## ETERNAL

To last forever; something or someone that has no beginning or end.

## GENTILE

A non-Jewish person.

## GLORY

Splendor and high honor.

## GOSPEL

**1.** The good news that God became flesh in Jesus, dwelt among us, fulfilled the Law given to us through Moses, paid the penalty for our sins with His death on the cross, and rose again on the third day so that we could be redeemed and restored to God. **2.** "Gospel" or "Gospels" describe one or more of the firsthand accounts of Jesus and His ministry (e.g., Matthew, Mark, Luke, and John).

## GRACE

God's unmerited favor toward sinners.

## HOLY/HOLINESS

To be set apart and pure. When referring to God, holiness is God's goodness, power, and majesty.

## INCARNATION

The process by which Jesus took on human flesh and became completely human while maintaining His full deity.

## INTERCESSION

To act on behalf of another. In the Old Testament, the priests interceded for God's people by making sacrifices on their behalf. On the cross, Jesus interceded for mankind by offering Himself as a sacrifice on behalf of mankind. Believers today intercede for other believers primarily by praying for them on their behalf.

## MERCY

God's kindness and readiness to forgive, demonstrated through the salvation He gives believers through Christ.

## PROMISED LAND

The land God promised to the Israelites where they would build their home and nation.

## REDEMPTION

The process at the time of salvation by which Christ's grace delivers believers from the bondage of sin and gives them freedom in Christ.

## REPENTANCE

The act of both confessing and turning away from sin in order to pursue obedience to God.

## RESURRECTION

The process by which someone who is dead is brought back to life.

## REVELATION

The act of revealing; to make something or someone known.

## RIGHTEOUS/RIGHTEOUSNESS

To do and be what is morally just and right. The standard of righteousness is God, who is perfectly righteous. In Christ, we receive His righteousness in the place of our unrighteousness, causing us to be declared righteous in God's eyes.

## SACRIFICE

An offering to God to give Him thanks or make atonement for sin.

## SANCTIFICATION

The process of becoming holy—becoming more like Christ. We go through this lifelong process after accepting Jesus as our Lord and Savior.

## SAVIOR

A title given to Jesus that describes Jesus as the One who ultimately provides salvation.

## SCRIPTURE

In the New Testament, the Scriptures referred to the Law and Prophets of the Old Testament, but today, Scripture refers to God's Word as a whole—the Bible.

### SIN

To miss the mark of obedience to God; to do, speak, or think anything that goes against God's law.

### SOVEREIGNTY

God's complete control over all things and His ability to operate in and through creation as He so wills.

### TABERNACLE

The portable place of worship in the Old Testament where God's presence would come to dwell with His people and where sacrifices were made out of thanks to God and for the forgiveness of sin.

### TEMPLE

The building first built by King Solomon and rebuilt over the centuries where God's presence would come to dwell with His people, where sacrifices were made out of thanks to God and for the forgiveness of sin, and where people would gather to pray and learn from the Scriptures.

### THE CHURCH

"The Church" (with a capital *C*) refers to all of God's people as a whole, whereas the terms "church" or "churches" (with a lowercase *c*) refer to local congregations made up of a portion of believers.

### THE LAW

The Law refers to the collection of laws, or instructions for living, that God established for the people of Israel in the Old Testament. The Law was composed of moral, civil, and ceremonial laws that the people were to obey in order to please God and be formed into God's holy people.

### TYPE/TYPOLOGY

A kind of analogy that the Old Testament uses to point to Christ. A "type" is a person, object, or institution that serves as a shadow, pointing forward to the true substance of Christ. An Old Testament "type of Christ" has similarities and differences to Christ, showing how the former is always an insufficient representation of the latter and thus points to Jesus as the true and better fulfillment.

*We see the promises fulfilled. Jesus has come once, and He will come again. This time, we wait in confidence.*

# THE ATTRIBUTES OF GOD

## Eternal

God has no beginning and no end. He always was, always is, and always will be.

HAB. 1:12 / REV. 1:8 / IS. 41:4

## Faithful

God is incapable of anything but fidelity. He is loyally devoted to His plan and purpose.

2 TIM. 2:13 / DEUT. 7:9 / HEB. 10:23

## Good

God is pure; there is no defilement in Him. He is unable to sin, and all He does is good.

GEN. 1:31 / PS. 34:8 / PS. 107:1

## Gracious

God is kind, giving us gifts and benefits we do not deserve.

2 KINGS 13:23 / PS. 145:8
IS. 30:18

## Holy

God is undefiled and unable to be in the presence of defilement. He is sacred and set-apart.

REV. 4:8 / LEV. 19:2 / HAB. 1:13

## Incomprehensible and Transcendent

God is high above and beyond human understanding. He is unable to be fully known.

PS. 145:3 / IS. 55:8–9
ROM. 11:33–36

## Immutable

God does not change. He is the same yesterday, today, and tomorrow.

1 SAM. 15:29 / ROM. 11:29
JAMES 1:17

## Infinite

God is limitless. He exhibits all of His attributes perfectly and boundlessly.

ROM. 11:33–36 / IS. 40:28
PS. 147:5

## Jealous

God is desirous of receiving the praise and affection He rightly deserves.

EX. 20:5 / DEUT. 4:23–24
JOSH. 24:19

## Just

God governs in perfect justice. He acts in accordance with justice. In Him, there is no wrongdoing or dishonesty.

IS. 61:8 / DEUT. 32:4 / PS. 146:7–9

## Loving

God is eternally, enduringly, steadfastly loving and affectionate. He does not forsake or betray His covenant love.

JN. 3:16 / EPH. 2:4–5 / 1 JN. 4:16

## Merciful

God is compassionate, withholding from us the wrath that we deserve.

TITUS 3:5 / PS. 25:10
LAM. 3:22–23

## Omnipotent

God is all-powerful;
His strength is unlimited.

MAT. 19:26 / JOB 42:1-2
JER. 32:27

## Omnipresent

God is everywhere;
His presence is near
and permeating.

PROV. 15:3 / PS. 139:7-10
JER. 23:23-24

## Omniscient

God is all-knowing;
there is nothing
unknown to Him.

PS. 147:4 / I JN. 3:20
HEB. 4:13

## Patient

God is long-suffering and
enduring. He gives ample
opportunity for people
to turn toward Him.

ROM. 2:4 / 2 PET. 3:9 / PS. 86:15

## Self-Existent

God was not created
but exists by His
power alone.

PS. 90:1-2 / JN. 1:4 / JN. 5:26

## Self-Sufficient

God has no needs
and depends on
nothing, but everything
depends on God.

IS. 40:28-31 / ACTS 17:24-25
PHIL. 4:19

## Sovereign

God governs over
all things; He is in
complete control.

COL. 1:17 / PS. 24:1-2
1 CHRON. 29:11-12

## Truthful

God is our measurement
of what is fact. By Him
we are able to discern
true and false.

JN. 3:33 / ROM. 1:25 / JN. 14:6

## Wise

God is infinitely
knowledgeable and
is judicious with
His knowledge.

IS. 46:9-10 / IS. 55:9 / PROV. 3:19

## Wrathful

God stands in opposition
to all that is evil. He enacts
judgment according to
His holiness, righteousness,
and justice.

PS. 69:24 / JN. 3:36 / ROM. 1:18

# TIMELINE OF SCRIPTURE

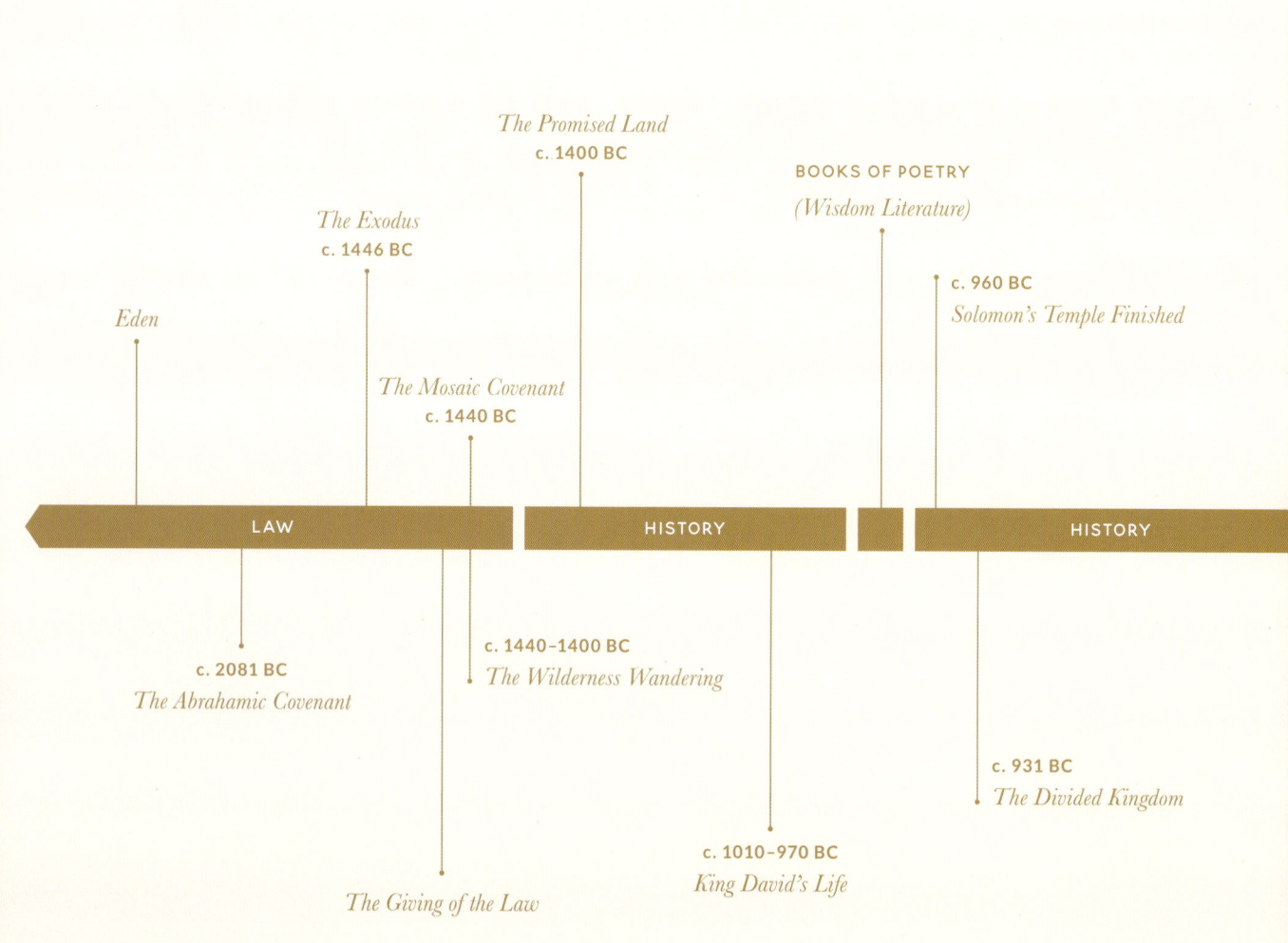

The Promised Land
c. 1400 BC

BOOKS OF POETRY
*(Wisdom Literature)*

The Exodus
c. 1446 BC

c. 960 BC
*Solomon's Temple Finished*

*Eden*

*The Mosaic Covenant*
c. 1440 BC

**LAW**

**HISTORY**

**HISTORY**

c. 2081 BC
*The Abrahamic Covenant*

c. 1440–1400 BC
*The Wilderness Wandering*

c. 931 BC
*The Divided Kingdom*

c. 1010–970 BC
*King David's Life*

*The Giving of the Law*

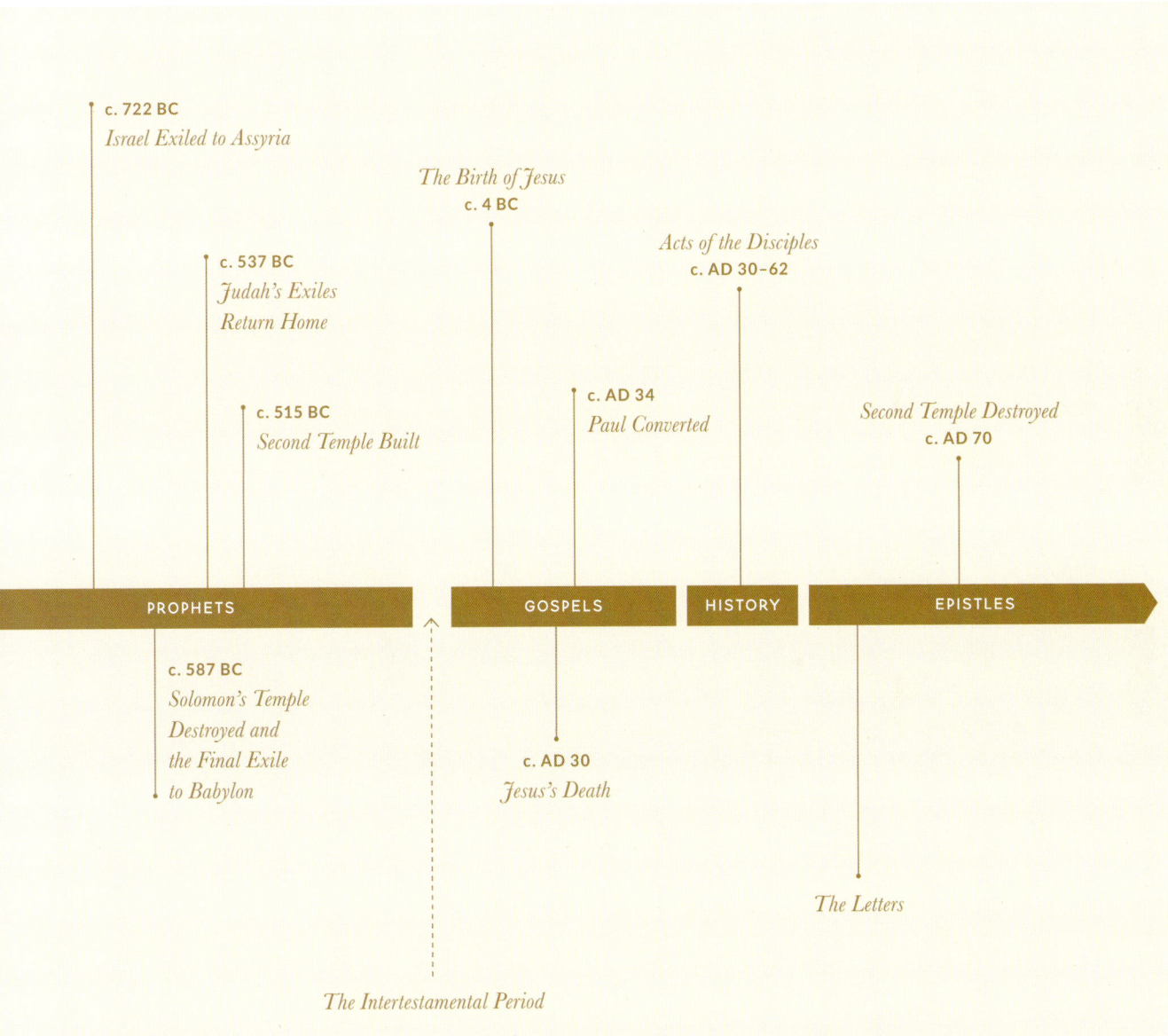

c. 722 BC
*Israel Exiled to Assyria*

*The Birth of Jesus*
c. 4 BC

*Acts of the Disciples*
c. AD 30–62

c. 537 BC
*Judah's Exiles
Return Home*

c. AD 34
*Paul Converted*

*Second Temple Destroyed*
c. AD 70

c. 515 BC
*Second Temple Built*

**PROPHETS**

**GOSPELS**

**HISTORY**

**EPISTLES**

c. 587 BC
*Solomon's Temple
Destroyed and
the Final Exile
to Babylon*

c. AD 30
*Jesus's Death*

*The Letters*

*The Intertestamental Period*

# METANARRATIVE OF SCRIPTURE

 *Creation* ⟶  *Fall*

In the beginning, God created the universe. He made the world and everything in it. He created humans in His own image to be His representatives on the earth.

The first humans, Adam and Eve, disobeyed God by eating from the fruit of the Tree of Knowledge of Good and Evil. Their disobedience impacted the whole world. The punishment for sin is death, and because of Adam's original sin, all humans are sinful and condemned to death.

##  Redemption

God sent His Son to become a
human and redeem His people. Jesus
Christ lived a sinless life but died on
the cross to pay the penalty for sin.
He resurrected from the dead and
ascended into heaven. All who put their
faith in Jesus are saved from death and
freely receive the gift of eternal life.

## Restoration

One day, Jesus Christ will return again
and restore all that sin destroyed. He
will usher in a new heaven and new
earth where all who trust in Him will
live eternally with glorified bodies in
the presence of God.

# WHAT IS THE GOSPEL?

*Thank you for reading and enjoying this study with us! We are abundantly grateful for the Word of God, the instruction we glean from it, and the ever-growing understanding it provides for us of God's character. We are also thankful that Scripture continually points to one thing in innumerable ways: the gospel.*

We remember our brokenness when we read about the fall of Adam and Eve in the garden of Eden (Genesis 3), where sin entered into a perfect world and maimed it. We remember the necessity that something innocent must die to pay for our sin when we read about the atoning sacrifices in the Old Testament. We read that we have all sinned and fallen short of the glory of God (Romans 3:23) and that the penalty for our brokenness, the wages of our sin, is death (Romans 6:23). We all need grace and mercy, but most importantly, we all need a Savior.

We consider the goodness of God when we realize that He did not plan to leave us in this dire state. We see His promise to buy us back from the clutches of sin and death in Genesis 3:15. And we see that promise accomplished with Jesus Christ on the cross. Jesus Christ knew no sin yet became sin so that we might become righteous through His sacrifice (2 Corinthians 5:21). Jesus was tempted in every way that we are and lived sinlessly. He was reviled yet still yielded Himself for our sake, that we may have life abundant in Him. Jesus lived the perfect life that we could not live and died the death that we deserved.

The gospel is profound yet simple. There are many mysteries in it that we will never understand this side of heaven, but there is still overwhelming weight to its implications in this life. The gospel tells of our sinfulness and God's goodness and a gracious gift that compels a response. We are saved by grace through faith, which means that we rest with faith in the grace that Jesus Christ displayed on the cross (Ephesians 2:8–9). We cannot save ourselves from our brokenness or do any amount of good works to merit God's favor. Still, we can have faith that what Jesus accomplished in His death, burial, and resurrection was more than enough for our salvation and our eternal delight. When we accept God, we are commanded to die to ourselves and our sinful desires and live a life worthy of the calling we have received (Ephesians 4:1). The gospel compels us to be sanctified, and in so doing, we are conformed to the likeness of Christ Himself. This is hope. This is redemption. This is the gospel.

# SCRIPTURES TO REFERENCE

**GENESIS 3:15**

*I will put hostility between you and the woman, and between your offspring and her offspring. He will strike your head, and you will strike his heel.*

**ROMANS 3:23**

*For all have sinned and fall short of the glory of God.*

**ROMANS 6:23**

*For the wages of sin is death, but the gift of God is eternal life in Christ Jesus our Lord.*

**2 CORINTHIANS 5:21**

*He made the one who did not know sin to be sin for us, so that in him we might become the righteousness of God.*

**EPHESIANS 2:8–9**

*For you are saved by grace through faith, and this is not from yourselves; it is God's gift — not from works, so that no one can boast.*

**EPHESIANS 4:1–3**

*Therefore I, the prisoner in the Lord, urge you to walk worthy of the calling you have received, with all humility and gentleness, with patience, bearing with one another in love, making every effort to keep the unity of the Spirit through the bond of peace.*

# BIBLIOGRAPHY

*Week 1*

Baldwin, Joyce G. *Tyndale Old Testament Commentary: Haggai, Zechariah and Malachi.* Vol. 28.
    Downers Grove: InterVarsity Press, 1972.

Carson, D. A. *The Gospel according to John.* The Pillar New Testament Commentary.
    Grand Rapids: William B. Eerdmans Publishing Company, 1991.

Grudem, Wayne A. *Tyndale Old Testament Commentary: 1 Peter.* Vol. 17. Downers Grove:
    InterVarsity Press, 1988.

Guthrie, Donald. *Tyndale Old Testament Commentary: Hebrews.* Vol. 15. Downers Grove: InterVarsity
    Press, 1983.

Kranz, Jeffrey. "The Beginner's Guide to the Prophets in the Bible." Overview Bible.
    October 3, 2019. https://overviewbible.com/prophets/.

Kruse, Colin G. *Tyndale Old Testament Commentary: John. Vol. 4.* Downers Grove: InterVarsity
    Press, 2003.

Ligonier. "Christ our Prophet." *Ligonier Ministries.* May 15, 2017. https://www.ligonier.org/learn/
    devotionals/christ-our-prophet.

Morris, Leon. *Tyndale Old Testament Commentary: Luke. Vol. 3.* Downers Grove: InterVarsity Press,
    1988.

O'Neal, Sam. "Who Were the Major Prophets in the Bible?" *Learn Religions.* February 23, 2019.
    https://www.learnreligions.com/introduction-to-the-major-prophets-in-the-bible-363402.

Storms, Sam. "What Does Scripture Teach About the Office of Prophet and Gift of Prophecy?"
    *The Gospel Coalition.* October 8, 2015. https://www.thegospelcoalition.org/article/sam-
    storms-what-does-scripture-teach-about-office-prophet-gift-prophecy/.

Thompson, J. A. *Tyndale Old Testament Commentary: Deuteronomy. Vol. 5.* Downers Grove:
    InterVarsity Press, 1974.

TOW Project. "Introduction to the Prophets." *Theology of Work Project.* Accessed May 11, 2022.
    https://www.theologyofwork.org/old-testament/introduction-to-the-prophets.

Walton, John and Andrew Hill. "Who Were the Minor Prophets?" Zondervan Academic.
    November 30, 2017. https://zondervanacademic.com/blog/minor-prophets.

## Week 2

Dennis, Lane T. and Wayne Grudem, ed. The ESV Study Bible. Wheaton, IL: Crossway, 2008.

Kimbrell, Joanna. *Search the Word: Knowing & Loving God through Intentional Bible Study.* Edited by Jana White and Alli Turner. Hanover, MD: The Daily Grace Co., 2020.

Mohler Jr., Albert R. *Christ-Centered Exposition Commentary: Exalting Jesus in Hebrews.* Edited by David Platt, Daniel L. Akin, and Tony Merida. Nashville: B&H Publishing Group, 2017.

## Week 3

Sproul, R. C. "The King Shall Come." Sermon. *Ligonier Ministries.* MP3 Audio. 20:29. https://www.ligonier.org/learn/series/coming-of-the-messiah/the-king-shall-come.

Sproul, R. C. "What Is the Kingdom of God?" *Ligonier Ministries.* September 13, 2021. https://www.ligonier.org/learn/articles/what-is-kingdom-god.

Strauss, Mark L. *Four Portraits, One Jesus: A Survey of Jesus and the Gospels.* Grand Rapids: Zondervan Academic, 2020.

## Week 4

Alexander, T. D. "Jesus as Messiah." *The Gospel Coalition.* Accessed November 14, 2022. https://www.thegospelcoalition.org/essay/jesus-as-messiah/.

Blue Letter Bible. "Lexicon: Strong's H4886 - māšaḥ." *Blue Letter Bible.* Accessed November 15, 2022. https://www.blueletterbible.org/lexicon/h4886/csb/wlc/0-1/.

Blue Letter Bible. "Lexicon: Strong's G5547 - christos." *Blue Letter Bible.* Accessed November 15, 2022. https://www.blueletterbible.org/lexicon/g5547/csb/tr/0-1/.

Mathison, Keith. "The Davidic Covenant—The Unfolding of Biblical Eschatology." *Ligonier Ministries.* March 5, 2012. https://www.ligonier.org/learn/articles/davidic-covenant-unfolding-biblical-eschatology

Welchel, Huge. "Magi and the Eternal Effect of Our Work." *The Gospel Coalition.* December 30, 2013. https://www.thegospelcoalition.org/article/the-magi-and-the-eternal-effect-of-our-work/

Youngblood, Ronald F, ed. *Nelson's Illustrated Bible Dictionary.* Nashville: Thomas Nelson, 2014.

Thank you for studying
God's Word with us!

CONNECT WITH US
@thedailygraceco
@dailygracepodcast

CONTACT US
info@thedailygraceco.com

SHARE
#thedailygraceco

VISIT US ONLINE
www.thedailygraceco.com

MORE DAILY GRACE
The Daily Grace® App
Daily Grace® Podcast